LIVING WITH STIGMA

The Plight of the People Who We Label Mentally Retarded

By

JAMES R. DUDLEY, Ph.D.

School of Social Administration
Temple University
Philadelphia, Pennsylvania

With a Foreword by
Lynn Wikler, Ph.D.
University of Wisconsin
Madison, Wisconsin

CHARLES C THOMAS • PUBLISHER
Springfield • Illinois • U.S.A.

Published and Distributed Throughout the World by

CHARLES C THOMAS • PUBLISHER
2600 South First Street
Springfield, Illinois 62717

© *1983 by* CHARLES C THOMAS • PUBLISHER

ISBN 0-398-04831-2

Library of Congress Catalog Card Number: 83-345

Printed in the United States of America
Q-R-1

Library of Congress Cataloging in Publication Data

Dudley, James R.
  Living with stigma.

  Bibliography: p.
  1. Mentally handicapped—Attitudes. 2. Mentally handicapped—Psychology. 3. Prejudices. I. Title.
RC570.D8 1983   362.2'042   83-345
ISBN 0-398-04831-2

LIVING WITH STIGMA

FOREWORD

MENTALLY retarded people do not write autobiographies. Nor do they often encounter sympathetic listeners to whom their story might be told. There are, of course, legions of people, all with advanced degrees, whose job it is to deal with the retarded and presumably also to listen to them, but these people have been taught to listen only to experts. Retarded people may in fact be experts about the conditions of their own lives, but they do not project the kind of expert image that commands attention.

The perspective of the retarded citizen, therefore, remains a private one, largely unknown to even the most concerned members of the population. This has long been the case. Until recently, many of us felt that we could safely ignore what the retarded might have to say (if indeed we suspected that they had any information new to us). Retardation was a problem for specialists, to be addressed largely within the confines of institutions that segregated the retarded from the rest of us with high walls of brick and mortar.

Fundamental changes in the sociopolitical landscape, marked by a long series of historic judicial rulings, brought about an end to the segregation approach. Deinstitutionalization brought the retarded to us, making it even more urgent that their voices be heard.

In this fine monograph, Jim Dudley provides a forum for these voices, giving us a revealing picture of what it is like to experience mental retardation as a member of contemporary American society. As his ethnographic data amply demonstrate, the physical walls of the institution have been replaced not by social integration but by an equally isolating, and demeaning, social barrier, a wall constructed of attitudes and be-

havior. The retarded person, once identified as such, is subjected to a systematic process of stigmatization that saddles him
or her with an imagined set of undesirable attributes that may
bear little resemblance to his or her individual character.

Especially poignant are the protective responses of the retarded person, such as the attempt to differentiate the self from
the "worst" cases ("I am low but not low low"). The retarded
person in society soon learns to confront negative stereotypes
not only from others but also from within. Gradually, the retarded person learns to help his "captors" in building and maintaining the wall, for it provides at least the illusion of protection
from the rejection that typically follows upon attempts to make
contact with the world of normals. Within this enclosed society,
the retarded person makes strenuous efforts to "normalize," ad-
hering with religious devotion to middle-class norms of marriage, work, and property. Indeed, even the hostility of
normals to mental retardation is recreated, in the form of
scapegoating of the most retarded. Yet, Dudley's study shows
that those who adopt these practices are aware, at one level,
that they fail the acid test of normality, which is acceptance as
normal by normals. Attempts at equality do not bridge separation.

The attitudes of normals, however, are not the greatest bur-
dens of this social stigma. The actions that spring from the attitudes lead to serious and unfair curtailments in the range of
opportunities and the quality of life of the retarded. The pattern begins with routinely being ignored when offering advice
or statement of preferences, as if mental retardation prevented
the development of a robust set of wants or the ability to establish personal priorities, and it continues in the worst cases with
outright physical abuse, including surgical intervention to pre-
vent the retarded person from making his or her own choices
concerning reproduction.

Jim Dudley's study shows how it feels to be subjected to
these attitudes and practices. His is a picture ordinarily inac-
cessible even to the professional working with the retarded.

Dudley elicited personal testimony in a setting in which the retarded person did not fear that the "wrong" response might threaten the continuation of needed services. And, most importantly, he proves to have been a most sympathetic listener. It is my hope that this opportunity to gain access to the retarded person's world will be used by professionals and their educators.

This study goes beyond reporting, however, to providing suggestions for change. A crucial contribution of Dudley's analysis is the documentation of the ways in which the stigmatization and segregation of the retarded is brought about in part by the behavior of precisely those professional persons whose job it is to ease their transition to noninstitutional society. These findings should be taken to heart by all of these professionals. A rigorous self-searching is called for, and efforts to combat rather than exacerbate stigma should be considered a professional responsibility. The enormous sociocultural differences between the professionals and their clients, in income, social status, power and, often, race—not to mention education and mental acuity—make this responsibility difficult to discharge; the present study, however, helps to make it equally hard to ignore.

Dudley provides, in Chapter 6, an admirable set of directives for effecting changes. Careful training or retraining of professionals and appropriate education of the retarded themselves could, in his opinion, lessen the burden of the status of the retarded person. Though the reader may be pessimistic concerning the likelihood of significant change, given the pervasive influence of a harshly competitive society in which this social issue arises, his suggestions are based squarely on the data he has collected and deserve serious consideration by all with responsibility for easing the difficult entry of the retarded into the social world in which we all should share.

Dr. Lynn Wikler

PREFACE

IN the early 1970s, I was involved in planning for the institutional discharge of the first group of people returning to a major Eastern city from a state institution for the mentally retarded. This was the time when deinstitutionalization was just getting under way in many states. Because the movement was just beginning, there frequently emerged new issues and problems pertaining to the degree of preparedness of the people being discharged and the nature of the response needed by the community-based service system.

I was frequently involved with a particular set of problems that had not been given serious consideration until they began emerging. These problems revolved around the opposition raised by local citizens to people with mental handicaps moving into their neighborhoods. I found myself attending zoning hearings in which citizens challenged the establishment of new group homes because of their alleged noncompliance with residential zoning codes. Civic organization meetings and community-wide public hearings were also occupying my time, as debate and opposition were voiced there as well. Among professionals, my time was increasingly spent discussing and formulating strategies for involving local neighborhoods in decisions about where group homes would be established. I became intimately aware of a variety of strategies used by provider agencies, ranging from a clandestine approach in which the neighbors were not initially informed that their new neighbors were mentally handicapped to one in which neighbors were openly informed, educated, and if possible recruited as volunteers. Meanwhile, the citizens in some of the neighborhoods where new group homes were already established continued to reveal their misconceptions about mental retardation and their prejudices, fears, and general discomfort with their new neighbors. It became evident to me that deinstitutionalization would need to be more than just preparing the people who were being discharged from institutions; the community service system would have to be expanded to address problems of the community.

The next phase of my involvement in the deinstitutionalization movement was from the distance of an academic position. I had time to reflect on my earlier experiences and to juxtapose my own developing notions with the theoretical notions of others conducting research in this field. I was particularly affected by a more in-depth study of historical trends in the provision of care for people with mental handicaps. These trends revealed to me the almost total dependency of service provisions on the development of American society and its fluctuating views on mental retardation and other disabilities. The century of institutional care became, for me, a more visible backdrop for the complex problems then facing the people being discharged.

In an extensive search of the literature, I became puzzled and disturbed by the limited number of naturalistic studies conducted that illuminated the everyday lives of people with mental handicaps: what they were feeling and thinking, who they associated with, how they spent their time, and what problems they were encountering. Edgerton's *Cloak of Competence* (1967), which was conducted in the early 1960s, is a classic of such studies. This work introduced me to the significance of stigma in the lives of mentally handicapped people and to the ethnographic approach used to study this problem area. Other studies have followed Edgerton's work utilizing an ethnographic or participant observation methodology, and their findings have confirmed, expanded upon, and updated Edgerton's. I was surprised, however, that these studies were referred to by relatively few people working in this field while the *Cloak of Competence* remained a popular reference.

In the late 1970s, I conducted a participant observation study that focused on the stigma problems of twenty-seven people who were labeled mentally retarded (Dudley, 1979). I must admit that initially I was in doubt as to whether the study could be conducted utilizing subjects who had mental handicaps. My doubts were based on both the limited amount of prior research with mentally handicapped subjects and my own misconceptions about whether these people could adequately express themselves on the subject of stigma. However, these doubts were short-lived, as my initial contacts with some of the participants of the study quickly enlightened me to their capacity to understand and communicate.

This book presents the findings of that study. It is a portrayal of the stigma problems facing twenty-seven people and the effect that these problems have on their lives. The first chapter introduces the concept of stigma and its significance as a problem confronting the deinstitutionalization movement. This chapter also introduces the theoretical perspective of the study and reviews previous research on stigma.

The next four chapters present the findings of the study. Chapter 2 introduces overall findings that show the research participants as "captives" of a "mentally retarded world" that is segregated from the mainstream. Chapter 3 presents perhaps the most significant set of findings of the study: data vividly describing the research participants' keen consciousness of their stigmatic status. Their perceptions of their handicaps, the mental retardation label, their peers, and their encounters with other people are also presented.

Chapter 4 reveals the variety of ways in which stigma was promoted in the lives of the participants, based on what they reported and what was observed. Thirteen different types of stigma-promoting incidents are presented, involving strangers, acquaintances, staff members, neighbors, and others in interaction with the participants. Chapter 5 examines the different ways in which the participants responded to stigma. Response patterns vary from being largely defenseless to actively resisting stigma. Passing as a non-mentally retarded person and encouraging stigma promotion for secondary gains are also examined.

Empowering mentally handicapped people to confront and resist the stigma in their lives is the theme of Chapter 6. Based on the findings of the study, the chapter recommends several specific ways of helping people with mental handicaps to understand their social circumstances and to act on their own behalf. Chapter 7 describes how the study was conducted, including the methods of selecting the research participants, the nature of the research methodology, the procedures and instruments that were used, and the ethical safeguards.

The terminology that we use in referring to other people is in itself an important indicator of how much we value them. Indeed, as the study reveals, the words that we use to identify someone can themselves be a serious barrier to communication, thwarting our capacity to perceive him as he actually is. Therefore, an attempt has been made in this book to use alternative terminology when referring to the general population of people who are labeled mentally retarded. Partially in response to the wishes of some of the participants, they will not be referred to as *mentally retarded* or *mentally retarded people*. Instead, when a general reference is necessary, *people with mental handicaps* or *people labeled mentally retarded* will be substituted. Hopefully, these minor word changes will aid the reader in understanding the people who are the concern of this book.

In retrospect, I am intensely aware that people with mental handicaps have much to tell us about themselves and their lives. They need to be more fully heard by researchers, legislators, administrators, planners, practitioners, volunteers, family members, and neighbors. Moreover, the burden for insuring the expression of their views must shift to all of us who associate with them as we seek to learn and to improve our means of communicating with them.

JRD

ACKNOWLEDGMENTS

I AM grateful to many people for assistance and support in conducting this study and writing this manuscript. Among the people who have provided helpful consultation on the development of the study are Dr. Merle Broberg, Dr. Dennis Brunn, Dr. Robert Edgerton and members of his research team, and Dr. Erving Goffman.

Many people have assisted in the data collection efforts, including Ms. Leslie Rosenthal, Ms. Karen Schott, and Ms. Petra Johns. Also, the administrators and staff of the four affiliate agencies continually supported the efforts of the researchers and greatly facilitated the data collection activity.

For their helpful comments on the development of the manuscript, I am grateful to Dr. Will Richan, Mr. Bern Ikeler, Ms. Dana Henning, and Dr. Lynn Wikler. Mrs. Sheila Booker was a crucial aid in typing the final manuscript.

Important support and encouragement were provided to me at various points in my work by several people, but I am particularly grateful to Ms. Yona Rogosin, Dr. Albert Wilkerson, Ms. Marian Bruin, and Mrs. Miriam Druckman.

Most importantly, I am grateful to the twenty-seven people who opened their lives and themselves to me as research participants. They have provided the material for this book and hopefully will accrue benefits from its publication.

CONTENTS

PROLOGUE

Research Participant: *What will the title of your book be?*

Researcher: *Can you give any suggestions?*

Research Participant: *How about, "What a Person Who Is Slow Is Like." Don't put down, "How a Retarded Person Is." Don't put the title down like that.*

LIVING WITH STIGMA

Chapter 1

THE SIGNIFICANCE OF STIGMA

When my girlfriend, Bev, and I are in her neighborhood, walking down the street, the kids there say, "Look, here comes the retardate." Then they call Bev a retardate too. I tell them they are dummies. Actually, names can never hurt me, only sticks and stones. I go and tell their parents and they side with their kids. So I go get a policeman to stop it.

THIS statement was made by Paul, a thirty-one-year-old man with cerebral palsy who is considered mentally retarded. Paul has some difficulty walking and speaks with an obtrusive drawl. He has lived his entire life with his parents and currently works as a kitchen helper, after working many years in a sheltered workshop.

Paul is one of twenty-seven research participants in the study that is presented in this text (Dudley, 1979). Paul's statement illustrates a problem that he and the other participants experience regularly because they have mental handicaps. This problem is the stigma that is associated with their mental handicaps and inevitably accompanies them wherever they go.

The study is a portrayal of the lives of twenty-seven people who live in a major Eastern city. These people live within a complex web of personal relationships and social meanings, which significantly affect their existence. This social web, as perceived and experienced by these twenty-seven people, is the focus of the study.

Twenty-two of the participants are considered mildly retarded, and five are considered moderately retarded, based on available IQ scores. They range in age from twenty-one to forty-two years. None are married and almost all of them either live with their parents or reside in group homes. They are similar to the general population of people with mental handicaps in this metropolitan area in terms of their race, sex, socioeconomic background, and geographic location.

To document the lives of these twenty-seven people, extensive field notes were taken of observations and conversations that they had with field researchers who remained in close contact with each of them for an average of eleven months. The researchers accompanied them to restaurants, shopping centers, bowling alleys, night school, and many other places. They traveled extensively with them on public transportation throughout the city and visited them at their residences, work sites, social gatherings, and other agency-sponsored events.

The data collection process consisted of three fairly distinct phases. The first phase involved getting oriented: developing rapport with the participants, other clients, and staff members who worked with them and explaining the purpose of the study. In the second phase, which was the longest, the researchers observed and participated in many facets of the participants' lives. The final phase consisted of several informal conversations with each of them.

SOCIOPOLITICAL CONTEXT

While only nine of the twenty-seven participants have previously been institutionalized in state institutions for the mentally retarded, all are dependent to some degree on the nationwide deinstitutionalization movement that has returned thousands of citizens with mental handicaps from institutions to residential communities (Butterfield, 1976). During the 1970s, an array of community-based services was established (Bruininks et al., 1981), and these twenty-seven participants are clients and thus beneficiaries of this community-based system.

The deinstitutionalization movement is a long overdue response to the basic human rights and needs of a forgotten segment of our population. Indeed, it is an affirmation of their humanity and a mandate for them rightfully to claim their full citizenship in society. It offers a radical departure from the previous institutional era that existed for over a century (Deutsch, 1967). A separate physical existence is no longer the formidable barrier that it once was, as increasing numbers of people with mental handicaps are living in the community with unprecedented freedom, opportunity, and access to a normalized life.

The movement has been successful in its efforts to physically integrate people with mental handicaps into the community, as living quarters, classrooms, training centers, and recreational facilities have been among the primary targets of concern during the past decade. The community-based system has largely succeeded in manipulating this physical environment so that it now approximates the normal physical world. In addition, the system has made significant progress in teaching its clients the competencies needed to participate with some independence in their physical environment.

The social world that is intertwined with this physical environment is the next frontier for the movement. Relatively little has been accomplished in integrating people with mental handicaps into the social fabric of their communities. Their interpersonal relationships seem to be confined to other clients within the mental retardation system, with few if any meaningful associations developing with neighbors, fellow employees, civic volunteers, church and club members, and others in the community. Their employment and leisure activities are also usually segregated from the mainstream of society and confined to separate facilites. Social integration is far from a reality, as separate and segregated living patterns seem to be the predominant representations of the current state of deinstitutionalization.

The decade of the 1980s appears to be a pivotal one for this movement. Conceivably the present trend will continue, with the community-based service delivery system expanding and maintaining its position as the dominant one. However, another possible scenario is that the major problems currently confronting the movement will remain essentially unsolved, leading to its demise and the return of another institutional era.

One of these major problems, possibly the most formidable one facing the movement, is the resistance in the community to mentally handicapped people. In a number of neighborhoods across the country, an alarmist element has organized and at times has successfully prevented mentally handicapped citizens from moving into their midst (e.g. Lubin et al., 1982). These alarmed residents do not appear to be intentionally malicious but instead seem to carry deep-seated fears and prejudices, which emerge in their attempts to protect their neighborhoods from outside intrusion.

Some of the comments of an alarmed group of residents confronted with mentally handicapped neighbors serve as an illustration:*

"The mentally retarded will get hurt in our neighborhood. They may walk into the street, and get hit by a car."

"I don't want my child playing with the retarded. It may rub off."

"They need the protection of an institution."

"We don't want blacks [who are also mentally handicapped] in our neighborhood."

"Will they keep their homes in good condition?"

"Build a high fence around their backyards so that they won't interfere in our lives."

These alarmed residents may or may not reflect the values of mainstream society. A Gallup Poll (1976) suggests that attitudes toward people labeled mentally retarded are improving. According to this poll, 85 percent of those interviewed said that they would not object to six mentally retarded people occupying a home on their block. Furthermore, 74 percent of those polled indicated that they do not fear mentally retarded people. While these findings suggest that the general public may be developing a more humane perspective toward mental retardation, the views expressed in the poll were responses to hypothetical situations, not real ones, and it is suspected that a smaller percentage of the general public would be supportive of mentally handicapped neighbors if the situation actually arose.

---

*These comments were made to the author when he was involved in deinstitutionalization efforts in 1972 and 1973.

Prejudices and misunderstandings about mental retardation seem to be prevalent among personnel who work with mentally handicapped people as well. Blatt (1969) found that the attitude of the staff members that he encountered during his institutional visits was so dehumanizing toward the patients that it far outweighed all other deplorable conditions observed. Studies that have been conducted on professionals' attitudes toward people with mental handicaps tend to reveal negative attitudes as well. Most research pertaining to professional attitudes has involved teachers. Studies have shown that regular education teachers do not possess especially positive attitudes toward children who are labeled mentally retarded (Gottlieb, 1975). While very few studies have been conducted on the attitudes of physicians, psychologists, and social workers, a study by Begab (1970) of social work graduate students revealed a general lack of understanding of mental retardation and a tendency to prefer other client populations. Thus while studies on the attitudes of people who work with mentally handicapped people are limited in number, they tend to support the view that prejudices are prevalent within this group.

Misconceptions and prejudices about mental retardation pervade American society. No one living in the society is free of their effects, as we have all been socialized almost instinctively to treasure intelligence, physical attractiveness, and self-sufficiency, and the reality is that people who are labeled mentally retarded tend not to have these qualities. Because of this reality, we have been taught to perceive them as devalued people and perhaps as the most inferior group of people in society.

People with mental handicaps live within the physical world of normals,* but a transparent wall separates them from its mainstream. This wall is fortified by institutional

---

*"Normals" refers to people who fulfill the prescribed norms of society.

policies, structures, and practices and by individual attitudes and behaviors, which all serve to reinforce the supreme importance that our society places on intelligence and other qualities that people with mental handicaps lack.

THEORETICAL CONSIDERATIONS

The study essentially draws from sociology and anthropology for both conceptual and methodological guidance. These sciences are peripheral to research and practice in the field of mental retardation, as the field is primarily influenced by a bio-psychological perspective. This peripheral status can be explained in part by the chronic lack of interest shown by sociologists and anthropologists and the relative absence of pertinent knowledge contributed by them. However, their peripheral status is also the result of basic ideological differences between the bio-psychological and socio-anthropological perspectives. The former perspective views mental retardation as a fixed biological property residing in a person, while the latter perspective views it as a property bestowed by some people upon other people because they fail to meet the system's norms or standards (Mercer, 1973). Each perspective investigates the problems surrounding mental retardation with different values, knowledge, and intentions.

While relatively few sociologists and anthropologists have conducted research in this field, an important body of conceptual knowledge does exist. Becker (1973), Goffman (1963), Lemert (1972), Farber (1968), Dexter (1964), Mercer (1973), and Edgerton (1967) are among the significant contributors.

Concepts by five of these theorists were initially considered in this study in terms of their potential for elucidating meaning from the data collected. However, early in the data collection process an analysis revealed that Goffman's concept of stigma and Lemert's of secondary deviation were most relevant in contributing theoretical understanding to the data collected, and the other concepts were dropped from serious consideration at that time.

In *Stigma: Notes on the Management of Spoiled Identity*, Goffman (1963, p. 3) states that the term *stigma* refers to a personal attribute that is deeply discrediting because it deviates from the norms of a social group. However, stigma applies more to the social meanings that are ascribed by the social group to the attribute than to the attribute itself. For example, in the case of a person with Down's syndrome, stigma applies primarily to the stereotypes ascribed to Down's syndrome rather than to the bodily evidence of it.

On the other hand, the attribute itself is an important property in stigma-promoting processes, as it reveals visible signs or cues that the person is stigmatized. These manifestations of a stigmatic attribute are called "stigma symbols" (Goffman, 1963, pp. 43-51).

Goffman is especially effective in helping the reader understand the perspective of the person with the stigma, particularly in encounters with normals. The stigmatized person has a dual perspective of being either "discredited" or "discreditable" in various social situations. In the former case, he assumes that his differentness is known about by normals with whom he is in contact, and he concentrates his energies on tension management. In the discreditable situation, he assumes that his differentness is neither known about by those present nor immediately perceivable by them, and he concentrates on management of information about his stigmatic attribute so that he will not be exposed and rejected. Goffman calls this latter option "passing as a normal," and he suggests that it is a feasible option for stigmatized people in at least some of their social situations.

Lemert (1972) develops a different position. He suggests that there are two kinds of deviation, primary and secondary. Primary deviation refers to the original cause of the deviant attributes while secondary deviation refers to behavior that is instituted to cope with the problems created by societal reaction to the primary deviation. Lemert suggests that stigma-promoting processes usually cannot be successfully contained and that, on the contrary, they could be viewed as a solution to one's problems. The "positive side of a negative identity" could take many forms, e.g. an opportunity to have friends because they have similar attributes or gaining special attention as clients of a cadre of helping professionals. In brief, Lemert would view deviance research from the perspective that social processes create, maintain, and intensify stigma, while Goffman would give more attention to the processes that manage and mitigate stigma.

These two theorists take different views of the same general phenomenon and raise significant questions for research and practice. Among these questions are: Can stigma be significantly mitigated? Can some people with mental handicaps pass as normal to lessen the effects of stigma? Or is it more realistic to view the stigmatic attributes of most people with mental handicaps as conspicuously different and unalterable, leaving them with no choice but to adapt to them? Further, are there temporary solutions to the problem of being stigmatized?

An additional set of questions, moral in nature, also needs to be asked: Even if people with mental handicaps are capable of passing as normal, should they be encouraged? Will passing create more problems for them because they know that they are not normal? Lemert (1972, p. 87) suggests that as long as a person keeps trying to be what he knows he is not — a normal, his problem continues.

RESEARCH QUESTIONS

The study reported in this text considers all of the above questions as it attempts to understand the phenomenon of stigma and its impact on the lives of the twenty-seven participants. The specific research questions that provided the study with an organizational framework changed very little over the course of the study. They are as follows:

1. Are social processes that promote stigma evident in the daily experiences of the participants? What forms do these social processes take?
2. Are the participants aware of the stigma-promoting processes that involve them? To what extent are they aware, and how do they communicate their awareness?
3. What noticeable stigma symbols do the participants have? Are they aware of their stigma symbols? How do they describe them?
4. Do the participants attempt to influence stigma-promoting processes to their benefit? Are there identifiable patterns in the ways that they do this? If so, do these patterns reflect the findings of other studies?
5. Who are the participants' close associates? How is their network of associates related to stigma-promoting processes?
6. Do the staff members and agency structures of the mental retardation system participate in stigma-

promoting processes? If so, what forms do these processes take?

7. Are there significant variations in the findings based on the participants' race, age, sex, IQ score, socioeconomic background, agency affiliation, residential status, geographic location, prior institutionalization, or nature of stigma symbols?

8. How critical is the problem of stigma in the lives of the participants?

The design of the study is fully described in Chapter 7, including further characteristics of the research participants, the method of selecting the sample, the research instruments and procedures, the ethical safeguards, the mechanisms to maximize objectivity, and the data analysis procedure.

PRIOR RESEARCH

Few studies have sought detailed and comprehensive accounts, largely from their own perspectives, of the lives of people who are labeled mentally retarded. Two such studies will be reviewed in some detail here because of the significance of their findings, the nature of their research designs, their wide acclaim, and the foundation they provide for this study. Edgerton's *Cloak of Competence* (1967), conducted during 1960-61, was an ethnographic study of forty-eight adults who were labeled mildly retarded and had recently been discharged from Pacific Hospital, a large California institution for the mentally retarded. Approximately 80 percent of these adults were white, with the remaining being either Mexican-American or black. This population was selected from a larger discharged population because they were considered to have the best chance of success in independent city living. The study consisted of many informal interviews with the subjects and "as much participation as possible" in the lives of these forty-eight people, including trips to recreational areas, grocery shopping, sightseeing drives, visits in their homes, participation in housework, financial planning, parties, and visits to the homes of friends and relatives.

The discussions were informal, and the subjects were encouraged to speak at length about any topics they chose. Seven topics served to guide the discussions, including where and how the subject lived; making a living; relations with others in the community; sex, marriage, and children; spare time activities; perception and presentation of self; and practical problems in maintaining themselves in the community.

Edgerton (1967, pp. 144-150) found that problems of daily living, while critical, were less so than problems related to stigma. Entering the world outside the hospital involved a "bewildering array of demands for competence," which resulted in the subjects facing two related problems: denying to themselves that they are mentally retarded, and passing, so that others neither suspect that they are nor accuse them of being retarded. Detailed accounts illustrated why and how the subjects passed in critical circumstances, i.e. on the job, finding a mate, managing material possessions, and interpersonal relations.

The study also revealed that almost all of the subjects were dependent to some degree on "benefactors," normal people who helped them with their problems (1967, pp. 172-204). These benefactors included employers, spouses, lovers, close relatives, landladies, neighbors, and others. These benefactors served with various degrees of importance not only to assist the subjects with practical problems but also to assist them with passing and denial efforts. Most of the benefactors had explicit knowledge about the subjects' past institutionalization and/or mental retardation status and served to protect them from humiliation that could be inflicted by other normals. Edgerton concluded his study by stating that the "benevolent conspiracy" of benefactors protecting these citizens had been most significant in helping them maintain themselves in the community. Without these benefactors, it is doubtful that most of them would have survived.

In 1971-72, Edgerton and Bercovici (1976) conducted a follow-up study of thirty persons from the original sample. They collected the same kind of information as in the earlier study. The findings revealed that some of these people had improved, some had worsened, and some had remained the same over the ten-year period. The concerns with stigma and passing were found to be far less evident, as only five people in the sample gave evidence that this issue was still central. Benefactors played a less important role in sixteen cases, and eleven continued to need benefactors to the same degree. No one was more dependent on a benefactor. When asked to compare their life to a period "about ten years ago," most of the people said that they were happier or things were about the same. Edgerton and Bercovici concluded the discussion of their findings by saying that the mentally handicapped person's opinion about his success in social adjustment to the community needs to be given more attention and weight in future research.

Another qualitative study of people labeled mentally retarded is *The Forgotten Ones: A Sociological Study of Anglo and Chicano Retardates* by Anne-Marie Henshel (1972). The subjects of this study were seventy-nine adults who ranged in IQ scores from 45 to 80 and in age from nineteen to forty-five years. The sample included a fairly balanced composition of Anglos and Chicanos, married and unmarried, and females and males. These subjects were identified from a population of the Texas Rehabilitation Commission. All of the subjects lived in Austin, and none apparently had been previously institutionalized. Henshel postulated that four variables—ethnicity (Anglo or Chicano), marital status, sex of the subject, and nature of the marital relationship—were critrical to the subjects' lives.

Henshel used a semi-structured, in-depth interview approach that consisted of three interviews. Interviews focused on the subjects' family of origin, children, friends, neighbors, leisure activities, finances, material environment, employment, health, and self-perceptions. Henshel also made her own assessment of such things as the subject's appearance, his ability to pass as a normal, and the conditions of his neighborhood, dwelling, and furnishings.

Henshel concluded that IQ scores were less significant in determining the life patterns of the subjects than their ethnicity, marital status, and sex. Detailed accounts of the subjects' lives were presented and organized within these areas. The findings pertaining to ethnicity will be summarized here because ethnicity is a variable of particular relevance to this study (1972, pp. 100-135).

The Chicano retarded citizens were viewed as being more attractive than the Anglos even though they more frequently exhibited visible characteristics of retardation. The Chicanos more often evaluated themselves positively, although they seemed more frequently plagued with adversity. Generally they led more normal lives according to the standards of their subculture, as they received more support from their own ethnic group through extended kinship and friendship networks. The Chicanos dated considerably more than their Anglo counterparts and had more close companions with whom they shared recreational pursuits. While the contacts that all of the subjects had with neighbors were limited, the Chicanos tended to have more neighbors with whom they were in contact, and their frequency of contact was greater than that of the Anglos.

Henshel's findings suggest that ethnicity may be a crucial variable that influences the degree to which stigma-promoting processes occur. Passing and denial, the social consequences of being mentally handicapped identified by Edgerton, may not be as important for Chicanos and other minority subcultures having supportive kinship and friendship networks and greater acceptance of mental retardation.

No other comparable ethnographic studies of people with mental handicaps living in the community could be found in a literature search, except for ongoing research of the Socio-Behavioral Group directed by Edgerton* and a recent study by Heshusius (1981).

· One other study should be noted, however, because it focuses on the self-perceptions of people who are labeled mentally retarded, an important focus of this study. To examine this topic, Lorber (1974) utilized a qualitative approach in interviewing twenty adults who were labeled mildly retarded. Two basic questions were asked via extensive informal conversation: In your opinion, what is mental retardation: and What is it like to be mentally retarded? The resulting extensive narrative of conversa-

*Socio-Behavioral Group, Mental Retardation Center, School of Medicine, University of California, Los Angeles, 760 Westwood Plaza, Los Angeles, California 90024.

tions was analyzed utilizing content analysis. The responses to the first question led to the identification of eighteen different categories defining mental retardation, e.g. intellectual disability, physical disability, different from normal, dislikeable label. The responses to the second question resulted in the emergence of several central themes that are relevant to the findings of this study (1974, pp. 42-43). Among these themes are the following:

> To be mentally retarded is both to deny that one is mentally retarded and to have much difficulty doing this.

> There is a keen and direct awareness of important kinds of incompetence and of being inferior to the task of mastery of the environment.

> Various strategies used to lessen or remove the stigma of mental retardation are admitting to some deficit that is much less stigmatizing, stressing that others are worse off and are the real mentally retarded people, attempting to avoid the stigma by being overly accomodating, and trying to elicit statements from others that one is not mentally retarded.

The findings of Edgerton, Henshel, and Lorber generally support the findings of this study. Specific references will be made to these and other studies in the chapters that follow.

A most significant characteristic of all three studies is that people with mental handicaps were the primary sources of the data. They were, in effect, consultants on their conditions and social experiences. Unfortunately, this client population has not generally been an active consultant or participant in the deinstitutionalization movement. This is in direct contrast to other oppressed groups (e.g. blacks, women, senior citizens) who have discovered the central roles that they must play in their social movements in order for them to succeed. Thus, the question must be asked about people with mental handicaps as well. Are they capable of speaking for and representing themselves? Further, can they begin to assume a leadership role in the deinstitutionalization movement? Their social status may remain essentially unchanged without their active participation.

The chapters that follow attempt to consider these questions in a preliminary way by exploring the capabilities of the twenty-seven research participants in understanding and articulating their basic needs and social circumstances. These chapters present the stories of these people as they reported them and as they were observed.

INTRODUCTION TO THE RESEARCH PARTICIPANTS

These twenty-seven people are identified in the book by first names, which are fictitious. To acquaint the reader with each of them, a brief introduction is provided below.

Those Affiliated with Agency A

1. *Martin* is thirty-four years old. He is white, lives with his parents, and works as a maintenance helper for a small private organization. Martin has no obvious obtrusive physical or behavioral characteristics. He is labeled mildly retarded.

2. *Roger* is thirty-six years old, white, lives with his parents, and works for the government as a file clerk. Roger has no obvious obtrusive physical or behavioral characteristics and is labeled mildly retarded.

3. *Mary* is twenty-two years old, white, lives with her older brother, and works in a sheltered workshop. Mary stutters slightly and has extreme difficulty walking without assistance. She has cerebral palsy and is labeled mildly retarded.

4. *Hank* is twenty-two years old, white, lives with his parents, and works in a sheltered workshop. He has a serious speech impediment and talks with a drawl. He also has limited vision and walks clumsily. He is labeled mildly retarded and formerly lived in an institution.

5. *Noreen* is twenty-seven years old, white, lives with her parents, and works for the government running errands. She has no obvious obtrusive physical or behavioral characteristics. She is labeled mildly retarded.

6. *Jenifer* is thirty-nine years old, white, lives with her father, and does not work. She has no obvious obtrusive physical characteristics but is extremely self-centered in conversations. She is labeled mildly retarded.

7. *Jim* is thirty-three years old, white, lives in a one room apartment near his parents, and works for the government as a manual laborer. He has no obvious obtrusive physical or behavioral characteristics and is labeled mildly retarded.

8. *Jill* is twenty-six years old, white, lives with her mother, and works in a sheltered workshop. She has no obvious obtrusive physical or behavioral characteristics. She is labeled mildly retarded.

9. *Nancy* is twenty-seven years old, white, lives with her parents, and works for the government as a file clerk. Her body proportions are noticeably abnormal with her torso being unusually large. She is la-

beled mildly retarded.

10. *Eugene* is twenty-seven years old, white, shares an apartment with another man, and works for a private company running errands. His most noticeable obtrusive characteristics are his boyish facial and body features. He is labeled mildly retarded.

11. *Paul* is thirty-two years old, white, lives with his parents, and works as a kitchen helper for the government. He has a speech impediment and talks with an obtrusive drawl. He also walks with an awkward gait. He has cerebral palsy and is labeled mildly retarded.

12. *Phillip* is twenty-eight years old, white, lives with his father, and works as a messenger for the government. He has a tendency to have temper tantrums and to smile in inappropriate situations. He is labeled mildly retarded.

13. *Susan* is twenty-five years old, white, lives with her parents, and is a file clerk with the government. She has a noticeable speech problem, as she talks with a young girl's voice. She is labeled mildly retarded.

Those Affiliated with Agency B

14. *Ann* is twenty-eight years old, black, lives in a group home (Agency B), and works in a sheltered workshop. She talks very slowly and walks with an irregular gait. She is labeled moderately retarded and formerly lived in an institution.

15. *George* is forty years old, black, lives in a group home (Agency B), and works in a sheltered workshop. He has noticeable Down's syndrome characteristics and is labeled moderately retarded. He

formerly lived in an institution.

16. *Karen* is twenty-eight years old, white, lives in a group home (Agency B), and works as a medical aid in a hospital. She has no obvious obtrusive physical or behavioral characteristics. She is labeled mildly retarded.

17. *Janet* is twenty-two years old, black, lives in a group home (Agency B), and works as a nurses' aide in a nursing home for old people. She has no obvious obtrusive physical or behavioral characteristics and is labeled mildly retarded.

18. *Sol* is forty-two years old, white, lives in a group home (Agency B), and works as a kitchen helper at a restaurant. He is usually nonverbal or gives one-word answers to questions. He is labeled moderately retarded and formerly lived in an institution.

Those Affiliated with Agency C

19. *Ron* is thirty-five years old, white, lives in a group home (Agency C), and works in a sheltered workshop. He has a boyish appearance and is labeled mildly retarded. He formerly lived in an institution.

20. *John* is twenty-four years old, white, lives in a group home (Agency C), and works in a sheltered workshop. He has no obvious obtrusive physical or behavioral characteristics and is labeled mildly retarded. He previously lived in an institution.

21. *Scott* is twenty-five years old, white, lives in a group home (Agency C), and works at a sheltered workshop. He has no obvious obtrusive physical or behavioral characteristics and is labeled mildly retarded. He has resided in several institutions.

Those Affiliated with Agency D

22. *Dora* is thirty-one years old, black, lives in a group home (Agency D), and works in a sheltered workshop. Her body proportions are noticeably abnormal with her head, arms, and legs being unusually large. She is labeled mildly retarded.

23. *Helen* is twenty-six years old, black, lives in a group home (Agency D), and works in a sheltered workshop. She has a cleft palate and walks with an awkward gait. She is labeled mildly retarded.

24. *Doc* is twenty-two years old, black, lives in a group home (Agency D), and works in a sheltered workshop. He has only limited use of his legs and usually walks with crutches. He has cerebral palsy, is labeled mildly retarded, and formerly resided in an institution.

25. *Pete* is twenty-three years old, black, lives in a group home (Agency D), and works in a sheltered workshop. He has no obvious obtrusive physical or behavioral characteristics and is labeled moderately retarded.

26. *Wil* is twenty-one years old, black, lives in a group home (Agency D), and does not work. He has no obvious obtrusive physical or behavioral characteristics and is labeled moderately retarded. He formerly lived in an institution.

27. *Louise* is twenty-five years old, is Egyptian, lives in a group home (Agency D), and works in a sheltered workshop. She has no obvious obtrusive physical or behavioral characteristics and is labeled mildly retarded.

Chapter 2

TWO SEPARATE WORLDS

Susan: I plan to be like a normal girl someday.

THE findings of this study suggest that two worlds exist, a mentally retarded world and a normal world. These two worlds typically exist side by side as separate entities with only occasional points of intersection. The participants in this study are confined to the mentally retarded world.

They are not confined in a physical sense as is the case when people with mental handicaps are institutionalized. Rather the two worlds are divided on a social basis, and the participants in this study are set apart from other people by the stigma that is associated with their handicaps.

The participants have almost complete access to the physical world of the non-mentally retarded. To some extent they are in close physical proximity to a fairly wide spectrum of non-mentally handicapped people, perhaps more than at any previous time in their lives. They frequent fast food restaurants, department stores, movie theaters, and spectator sports events, but beyond these excursions that require little if any interaction with the public their visits into the normal world are infrequent and often not repetitive. They are usually pursued with caution and sometimes with trepidation.

Phillip's circumstances are illustrative. This participant had played table pool at his affiliate agency for many years and had become so skilled at playing the game that he emerged as the best player at the agency, playing better than the staff members as well as the clients. One day he announced that he had joined a table pool club in his neighborhood and would not be playing pool so frequently at the agency. Months passed, and then he was asked about his membership with the club. His response was that he had gone to the club only a couple of times and discontinued going. He said that he preferred playing table pool alone at home. He offered no reason for his change of plans, but the reason seemed obvious: he felt unaccepted at the pool club.

The participants' physical world is largely confined to the settings where they reside, work, and receive services from the mental retardation system. In many cases their residences and day activities are also administered by the mental retardation system, and thus their physical world is often confined to the settings of this system.

Generally the participants look to the people and programs within these settings for the fulfillment of their needs. For example, many of the participants affiliated with Agency A, a multiservice agency, say that they would have no other place to go to meet people if this agency did not exist. They say that their time would be spent staying home and doing nothing other than watching television if they did not partake in the activities sponsored by this agency, which provides to people with mental handicaps an array of leisure and recreational services that is not available elsewhere in the metropolitan area. The generic agencies providing similar services, such as a YMCA or a social club, are in most cases not utilized by the participants, and in the few cases that they are utilized, the participants have concluded after one or two visits that they do not feel comfortable returning to them.

The participants and their associates are not uninterested in socializing. To the contrary, whenever opportunities for them to socialize within the mental retardation system are provided, they eagerly take advantage of them. Their need for leisure and social contacts is evident in their faithful attendance at most scheduled social events. It is also evident in their persistent attempts to interact with each other at virtually all of the activities they attend as clients, irrespective of the programs' objectives. For example, a night school program that is attended by a number of the participants appears to serve more as a gathering place for socializing with past and present friends and acquaintances than as an academic program. Often the night school provides the only opportunity for these people to meet with one another. The sheltered workshops also seem to serve as gathering places where friends can meet, pursue romances, and catch up on the news of other people in their common network of acquaintances.

In almost every instance, the participants have other mentally handicapped people as close friends. They are roommates in group homes, members of the same special clubs, fellow trainees at workshops, and associates from previous programs. Sometimes these personal associations are long-standing ones that originated many years before in a shared institutional experience. Although deinstitutionalization may have moved them in divergent directions, the friends still attempt to maintain contact in a common workshop experience or through periodic phone calls.

During the conversation phase of the study, the participants were asked to identify the people to whom they felt closest. Their responses revealed that most of their close associates are mentally handicapped people (a total of eighty-five people) and that most of these are clients of the same affiliate agency as the participants (seventy people). Thirty other people were identified by the participants as close associates. Twenty-one of them are either staff members working for the mental retardation system or family members and friends of their families.

The remaining nine non-mentally handicapped people who were identified as associates are significant in that they represent people outside the mentally retarded world. Six participants identified them as close associates, even though (with one exception) they seem to have only peripheral relationships with these people. The participants admit seeing them very infrequently, at times only once or twice, and the nine people generally do not appear to have much investment in the relationship. For the participants, then, these relationships may have their greatest meaning as symbols of what they want and do not have — friendships in the outside world.

THE WALL

The wall dividing the participants from non-mentally retarded people derives from their bio-psychological handicaps. Their handicaps stand in the way of their being normal people, even though their handicaps are not in themselves formidable. Actually, they vary to a striking degree in their nature and severity. Some participants have obtrusive physical deformities that are unappealing. A speech drawl, a noticeable limp, uncontrollable body movements, and childlike facial features characterize several participants, while others have no noticeable physical abnormalities.

All twenty-seven participants exhibit some form of intellectual impairment. Some cannot readily comprehend

conversation in abstract form. Some are preoccupied with
conversation that revolves around themselves and will not
even partake in other conversation. Some are slow in re-
sponding to all inquiries. Some seem to have limited
problem-solving capacities and cannot easily follow the
common sense progression that moves from understanding a problem to taking some action to alleviate it. Many
of the participants, however, revealed themselves to be
quite astute intellectually, particularly as the researchers
became better acquainted with them. A few can carry a
conversation on almost any subject, and some demonstrate unusual insights into their circumstances.

Besides physical and intellectual handicaps, many of
the participants also exhibit emotional problems, which
in most cases are a secondary derivative of their physical
and intellectual handicaps. These problems often become
most noticeable when they relate to others. Most of the
participants lack assertiveness in expressing their needs,
and a few are extremely shy and withdrawn. Some behave inappropriately while interacting with others by in-
truding into the other person's private space with
unwanted physical contact or conversation. These participants lack the sensitivity needed to understand subtle cues
communicating that that is unacceptable behavior. Almost all of the participants are misinformed in their attitudes toward sex and sexual behavior. Very few reported
that they have ever experienced sexual intercourse.

These bio-psychological handicaps, however, are not
the primary cause for the existence of their separate
world. The participants' handicaps are quite diverse, and
yet every one of them is set apart from the world of normals. What they have in common is the stigma that is associated with their handicaps.

Stigma refers to the negative social meanings that accompany them because their handicaps deviate from such cherished societal norms as intelligence and attractiveness. Because of these deviations, the normal world does not value their presence and participation in it and, to the contrary, responds unsympathetically, insensitively, and at times harshly to their struggles to survive and improve their lives.

The participants are keenly aware of the negative meanings that society associates with their handicaps. They believe that they are stigma carriers, and each additional experience with others that is demeaning, rejecting, or otherwise insensitive simply reinforces this belief. Each negative experience is a painful reminder of what they suspect they will encounter on future visits to the outside world.

The participants have in a sense helped to maintain the wall that divides them from others, as they almost instinctively suspect that a normal will view them as an inferior, and they seem to look intently for evidence that will substantiate this suspicion. They choose to stay in their confined world because they sense that the rejections on the outside will be too painful for them to face. They are caught up in a vicious cycle of experiencing rejection, suspecting further rejection, and retreating to the safe grounds of their protective world. Their retreat only increases their isolation from normals and thus widens the division between them.

The findings of this study describe the confined world of the participants. Within this world there is often an atmosphere of discontentment, particularly among the higher functioning people. These people are keenly conscious of their superiority over their lower functioning peers, and this consciousness sometimes leads them to reject and scapegoat these peers in ways similar to the ways that they are treated by non-mentally handicapped people. They are also discontented with the restrictions imposed on their relationships with normals. Some of them have made attempts to establish relationships with normal people only to be pushed away.

The participants and their peers wish to be normal people. They seem to consistently behave as respectable, law-abiding citizens, and they express normal aspirations. A discussion of a rap group involving five of the participants and ten other clients illustrates their aspirations. The leader of the rap session asked the members to share their most important personal goals, and their responses were to be employed, to earn a decent salary, to have their own homes, to take care of themselves, to get married, and to have their own children. Every member of the group mentioned at least one of these goals, and no one identified a personal goal that could be construed as socially unacceptable.

The identification of the participants with the norms of society is probably no different from that of most Americans, except that the participants seem to spend an excessive amount of their time and energy thinking about and discussing these aspirations. They are so intensely preoccupied with being self-sufficient, married, and normal because the obstacles to these goals seem overwhelming if not insurmountable.

The obstacles to achieving normal aspirations are in part a direct result of the physical and intellectual limitations imposed by the participants' handicaps, but they also derive in important ways from the stigma that is associated with their handicaps. The more that the participants perceive themselves as stigmatic, the less self-confident they seem to be in considering normal aspirations, and concomitantly the more obsessed they become with the wish to be normal.

This obsessive wish is sometimes manifested as a pretentious presentation of their normal attributes. The circumstances surrounding Roger's decision to get married illustrate the point. When he became engaged, the news of his marriage spread quickly throughout his agency's client membership because his fiancée is not labeled mentally retarded. Most important to the clients was that she is a normal person. One day Roger brought his fiancée to the agency to introduce her to others and in a sense to show her off, as he went out of his way to introduce her to everyone present. Ironically, she appeared to be the least physically attractive woman present at the agency that day. However, her unattractiveness was less important than the normal status that she represented.

According to society, the image of being a person with a mental handicap is the antithesis of the image of being normal. It seems that a person is either stigmatic or not, mentally retarded or not, an outsider or an insider. There does not seem to be a continuum toward normality.

The participants, however, are not able to accept this dichotomy. They recognize that they are not normal, that they are different in certain respects from other people. But they are also adamant that they are not creatures of a different kind. They perceive themselves to be much more like other people than different from them. They know that their handicaps and the limitations they impose vary greatly, and most of them do not classify themselves as mentally retarded.

Nancy, who has struggled for a long time with the question of whether she is mentally retarded, finally decided, "I realize that I'm sort of what you call borderline.

I'm in the middle — not here and not there." And so it is with most of the participants. They are not mentally retarded, and they are not normal. Despite what others feel, they perceive themselves as being somewhere in between.

While most of the participants are noticeably discontented with life in the confined world of the mentally retarded, only a few of them were observed to be ready to leave it. The metaphor of a wall is an apt one in that the participants have to choose one world or the other. If there is a portal in the wall, it is not one that is available for frequent movement between the two worlds, but a one-way exit to the non-mentally retarded world. If the participants can get out, they realize that they have to stay out, i.e. disassociate themselves from the world left behind.

There seems to be no established portal for the participants to the non-mentally retarded world. While society has developed methods for labeling them and socializing them into a mentally retarded world, the methods for removing the label and disengaging them from that world seem largely nonexistent. Those who want to leave are faced with contriving their own exit or escape.

In summary, two worlds exist. The world of normals does not exist for the twenty-seven participants or for countless other people with mental handicaps. The next three chapters provide descriptive accounts of these twenty-seven participants. These accounts reveal their perceptions of and experiences in the mentally retarded world and their means of coping with a separate existence.

Chapter 3

THE KEEN CONSCIOUSNESS
OF THE STIGMATIZED

Jim: I won't say I am smart when I am not. I don't mind telling people I am slow.

A PREVALENT view among the general public is that people with mental handicaps are limited in their emotional capacity as well as in their intellect. More specifically, people often believe that mentally handicapped people neither understand nor suffer from the adversities associated with their handicaps. The myth is sometimes expressed as, "Those poor, unfortunate people! Thank God that they don't know their plight and thus don't have to suffer."

This view that people with mental handicaps are largely unaware of their personal and social circumstances exists even among people with whom they have close associations. Many staff members working in the mental retardation system operate from this premise. For example, when information is needed to assess what a client needs, the client is often not consulted as an important information source. Instead, his relatives and staff members are asked to evaluate his capacity to function or his readiness for a particular program. Even at times when the client's basic survival seems at stake, e.g. in class action suits pressing for deinstitutionalization, his role is usually insignificant, with others taking over the battle.

Research is also noticeably negligent in consulting people with mental handicaps. Problems of reliability and validity usually arise, deriving from the general premise that these people are not knowledgeable or reliable enough to be qualified as research subjects. Studies such as those attempting to determine how effectively clients have adjusted to community living, particularly after being institutionalized, end up using every reasonable indicator of success but the views of the people themselves.

This prevalent view that people with mental handicaps are largely unaware of their circumstances and their plight is being increasingly questioned by practitioners, researchers, family members, and others who know them. The findings of this study also clearly challenge this view, suggesting instead that adults with a mild or moderate level of retardation are very aware of their personal and social circumstances. The participants in this study, in most cases, are keenly aware of their handicaps, have strong views about whether or not they are mentally retarded, and perceive that they are stigmatized because of their handicaps.

AWARENESS OF THEIR HANDICAPS

All twenty-seven participants were asked whether they have a handicap and if so to describe it and the limitations that it imposes. All of the participants had views to share, and in most cases they are fairly accurate descriptions of their conditions.

Many of them simply see themselves as slower than others. For example, Karen explained, "I'm slow at times and it takes me three times longer than it would take someone else." Roger said, "I'm no different from the other guy. I can do what anyone can do. It just takes longer." Other participants view their handicaps as deficiencies in school-related subjects such as reading, writing, and mathematics. As Noreen explained, "I only have problems with reading, writing, and counting. I can do all of the housewife things . . . cook, sew, clean."

Some of the participants, those having a medically diagnosed condition such as cerebral palsy, view their handicap in terms of its physiological aspects. Mary explained, "I had encephalitis at 11 months and was damaged. Before that I was a normal, healthy child. I have cerebral palsy which has affected my right arm and left leg, which I haven't control of. I can't walk without a cane or someone holding my hand."

Other participants attribute their circumstances to earlier behavioral problems. John explained, "My behavior was backward before. I got into fights a lot." He says that in his case the reason that he was previously in a mental retardation facility was this behavioral problem, which his parents could not manage at home.

A few of the participants reveal more introspection when they talk about their handicaps. They go beyond labeling their handicap as a learning deficiency or physical disability by describing its nature and the influence that it has on their functioning. Eugene talked about himself this way, "I may be slow in certain things. I might not be slow in certain things. It depends, you know. Possibly I can maybe do something better than they do. I don't know. I don't think I'm good at arithmetic. I guess I could do better." Paul explained, "I feel like I don't have everything all right but I have grown a lot over the years. I can walk good some days and not others. I can think well some days and not others. When I can't, it's because I am upset, but usually I can carry a conversation with anyone."

Finally, some of the participants deny that anything is wrong with them. In these cases, they do not actually believe what they express about themselves; rather, their intent is to deny the existence of their handicap in an attempt to conceal this vulnerable aspect of their identity. Scott said, "The only thing wrong with me is that I had a kidney disease when I was born."

Ron said, "The only thing I see wrong with myself now is my weight. Now you may have lots of other thoughts." Martin's explanation: "I say I'm a human being. I can do what they [non-mentally handicapped people] can do. I can work for all my own money. Every day I could go to the bus. One man sat there, talk to me. I talk back to him."

In many cases the participants view their handicaps not as a fixed condition but as one that is diminishing in the degree to which it imposes limitations. This view often includes the admission that their handicap was once quite severe and debilitating but now seems milder and less significant, so that they feel significantly more favorable about themselves. For example, Paul said, "I have learned how to get along as I got older." Ron, while talking about his twenty-year residency at an institution, said, "I used to work seven to eight days in a row helping the cripples. One day I realized that I was not crippled or bent out of shape . . . I was a normal person and I didn't belong there."

Incorporated into almost every participant's view of his handicap is a sense of ambivalence about how debilitating it is. He is not sure how much to highlight the limitations that it imposes and how much to play it down as insignificant. The tendency seems to be to emphasize its insignificance. If the handicap can be labeled as a localized, physical disability such as a speech defect or as a specific learning deficit, it seems easier to accept and manage in relation to self-image.

THE MENTAL RETARDATION LABEL

To be viewed as a slow learner is one thing, but to be viewed as mentally retarded is something altogether different. Most of the participants will not introduce the term *mentally retarded*, nor will they openly volunteer their views about whether they see themselves as mentally retarded. But when asked that question in the study, their responses were usually quite revealing. Typically they seemed startled by the question, as if it were taboo, not to be mentioned. Sixteen of the twenty-seven participants denied that they were mentally retarded, three admitted that they were, and eight expressed some form of ambivalence or said that they did not know.

A closer examination of the responses of those who denied being mentally retarded reveals some of their feelings and views. Janet's response to the question was, "No . . . , I hate the word." Eugene, less angry, responded, "I don't think I'm retarded . . . I don't feel retarded." Karen explained, "No, I see myself as suffering from not starting at X school [a special school for the handicapped] in kindergarten." She did not begin to attend this school until the age of sixteen.

A number of the participants revealed in their responses *why* they do not view themselves as mentally retarded. Their comments were as follows:

Phillip: No, . . . maybe a couple of years ago, but not since I have a job.

George: No, I don't. I was at X institution but not

anymore . . . once in awhile I am mentally retarded.

Ron: No, I get up, go to work, work from eight to three, fix my own dinner, wash my dishes, don't answer to anyone.

Jenifer: I'm mildly retarded — why do they call me mentally retarded? That's for very low people.

Helen: No, a mentally retarded person cannot walk or talk. I can walk and talk.

Roger: When I think of the word *retarded*, I think of people who are vegetables. They can't do anything for themselves.

These participants reveal their definitions of mental retardation. They portray it as a pervasive debilitating condition in which a person is almost totally incapable of caring for himself, similar to conventional definitions of severe and profound retardation. In a sense, to many of the participants the label itself is a debilitation, as it seems to be associated with such socially undesirable qualities as dependency, incompetency, and being subhuman.

As stigmatic as the mental retardation label may be, some of the participants, having previously internalized it as part of their identity, equivocated in their responses to the question, for example:

Noreen: No, I don't see myself as retarded . . . maybe half retarded.

Susan: Not mentally retarded, mildly retarded.

Ann: Maybe I am, maybe I can't learn things, but I think it just takes me longer.

Jill: In some ways I'm retarded and in some ways I'm not. I'm afraid of people and don't like to get close . . . I'm afraid I will get treated bad as I did as a child.

Pete: I don't know, ask my teacher.

These participants are not sure whether the label fits them or not, yet their views on this topic were usually expressed with intense feelings, suggesting that this question is crucial to the more general question of who they are.

NEGATIVE SOCIAL MEANINGS ASSOCIATED WITH THEIR HANDICAPS

What is perhaps the most significant finding of this study revolves around the participants' awareness of the various negative social meanings that are associated with their handicaps. This awareness is at times intricately entwined in their conversations on other topics. A few of their conversations are illustrative. While talking about her dating life, Karen was discussing the initial reactions that two new acquaintances might have toward each other when they first meet. She was planning to go out with a man who was blind, and she said, "He won't really be able to see me. I wonder if he knows about 'you know' [her mental retardation]?" Jill, in referring to her dating life, said, "Men will not like me when they find out I am slow." Phillip revealed his awareness more subtly with, "I like women who work at my office but I wouldn't date them." When asked why, he said that they are either married or "higher educated" thus "don't want someone like me."

Often the words that the participants use in conversing are themselves revelations of awareness. Words such as "slow," "borderline," and "more advanced" are used to describe themselves and their peers. Negative references are often chosen to describe their lower functioning peers, e.g. "low," "lower," "down," "vegetable," and "goofy." They occasionally use words to distinguish themselves from non-mentally handicapped people, calling the latter "normals" and "outsiders." Two participants were observed incorporating this awareness into impulsive bursts of anger with "you raving idiot" and "that retarded bitch."

Stratification Issues

A topic that was of special interest to many of the participants revolves around the heterogeneity within their client population. The range of levels of mental functioning among people with mental handicaps is a fact of which most people are aware, but it has special meaning for many of the participants. Most of them function at a relatively high mental level. They are quick to point this out to outsiders and to stress that they are more like normal people than they are like lower functioning clients.

Martin explained it this way: "I am able to hold a job. Others at my agency are not because they are lower level." Susan's explanation was: "We're our own bosses and the others act like they're babies, but they're really not." Eugene confidentially told the researchers, "I almost didn't get into the agency initially because my IQ is a little higher than the others and I am smarter." In a final example, Mary seemed to get to the heart of the issue, saying, "I like the people at the agency who are at my level. The others I don't have much to do with. They are too low. Not low low, but low. I have nothing against retardation. That is their handicap. But I don't need to be subjected to it."

Beyond identifying the differences between themselves

and their lower functioning peers, some of the participants also express hostility, ridicule, and embarrassment. Roger and Phillip concurred that they would not date clients of their agency. One told the other, "You can't talk to them. I have to act goofy to be with them." These two participants relished recounting an experience at a recent agency-sponsored party. One joked to the other, "They [lower level clients] were grabbing all of the food as soon as it was served. One kept bumping into me while I was serving food. They acted like such babies!"

Paul shared his view with more perspective, "Some clients are twenty-one and their bodies are like eight-year-olds. They aren't retarded though. Their parents are retarded. They hold them back and won't let them go out on their own." John said in a moment of unguarded reflection, "I wish I had a girl friend who was smarter. It bothers me when someone calls my girl friend retarded.

Finally, Martin recalled an agency-sponsored trip that he attended. He said "They [lower functioning peers] were always fighting, yelling, or arguing. It was embarrassing. One of them called her boyfriend at five in the morning and woke up everyone in my room."

Lower functioning people and others with obtrusive handicaps are not desirable associates for many of the participants, particularly in public. In part, the participants choose their associates based on the effect that they will have on their social acceptability. Karen, in recalling a recent restaurant experience with her roommate, illustrated this. She recounted, "She [her roommate] kept bumping into the woman at the next table as she ate her salad." This infuriated Karen because she felt that her roommate was oblivious to what she was doing. She added, "Just because she is retarded, she doesn't have to act it."

One might think that the people who would be most sympathetic to persons with mental handicaps would be people with a milder degree of mental disability. After all, this latter group could feel fortunate that their handicaps are not so severe and limiting. The central reality of stigma in the lives of the participants, however, seems to overshadow a natural concern for what they may have in common. Lower functioning people are too similar in identity to be considered close associates.

Problems in Agency Affiliation

Just as associations with other people could be viewed as problematic, associations with particular programs, living arrangements, and agencies create problems as well. Sometimes, mere affiliation with an agency creates a problem. Some of the participants are aware of this, as Janet, who is enrolled in a special night school program, illustrates. After meeting a handsome male visitor at her school program, she commented on how attractive he was and then added, "He is going to think that I am stupid because I go to a dumb school." Karen, with similar awareness, is upset because her dates do not ask her out again once they discover that she lives in a group home.

In most cases, the programs of the agencies observed in the study are appropriate for adults and relevant to the needs of the clients that they serve. However, some of the programs seem to promote unnecessary dependency and childlike behavior and fail to adequately challenge the clients. The participants are particularly aware of these programs and the negative factors associated with being affiliated with them. The sheltered workshop programs are by far the most notable example of such programs. Thirteen of the participants were affiliated with sheltered workshops while the study was being conducted, and eleven additional participants had previously worked at workshops.

Some of the comments of participants about their workshop experiences reveal their views.

Noreen: I hated it.

Phillip: I was lucky to leave that workshop after only a six-month stay. Some stay for two to three years.

Mary: It [workshop] stinks. My job involves putting screws in a bag, stuffing envelopes . . . It makes me feel like I'm retarded.

Two participants who have never worked in a sheltered workshop have similar views. Martin said, "Thank goodness I never had to work in one of them." Eugene said, "I looked at one but would never go in there. I looked at X workshop, I felt higher than that. I'm stuck in the middle . . . I'd rather stay home than go to a workshop." Two other participants feel so strongly about not working in a sheltered workshop that they advised their peers against it. Paul said to another participant, "Get wise, leave the workshop and get a real job." Phillip, in speaking to a group of clients in a day program about his job with the city government, concluded with the advice, "Take any job to get out of this program."

Some of the complaints about sheltered workshops explain why these people are so adamant in their views. Ron explained, "Usually they don't have anything for us to do, and I still have to go every day. It makes me angry that I have to go to work and then there is nothing to do." Hank reflected on a previous workshop experience, saying, "I could do better. Putting a sponge in a paper bag . . . I could do more than that. Others might need it though." Some complained because they make so little money. Roger, a former trainee of a sheltered workshop, erupted with anger while recalling his experience. "I was kept down. When I tried to advance to a higher level of work, I was changed to another job. The staff there wouldn't let me talk for myself. I was working for pennies."

As these illustrations point out, the type of work, the inadequate advancement opportunities, and the meager salaries partly explain why the workshops are despised by many of the participants. It is also suspected that the heterogeneity of the client population is a problem for those who are more stigma conscious. Furthermore, the underlying fear of never being able to leave a workshop and hold a job in the normal world is a preoccupation of some of the participants.

Variations in Awareness

All but two of the twenty-seven participants expressed awareness of negative social meanings associated with their handicaps. However, there are some significant variations among the participants in the frequency and form of their expressions.

The participants' expressions of awareness varied significantly by agency affiliation. Participants affiliated with Agencies A and B expressed stigma awareness approximately five times more frequently than those affiliated with C and D. Two particular areas in which this was most evident were preoccupation with stratification issues and open recognition of one's handicap and the stigmatic factors associated with it.

The client populations of Agencies A and B are heterogeneous in level of functioning,* with some clients functioning at significantly higher levels than others. In contrast, the client populations affiliated with the other two agencies, C and D, are much more homogeneous. This suggests that the more heterogeneous the peer group of the participants, the more frequent is their expression of (and preoccupation with) stigma awareness.

All of the participants affiliated with Agency C expressed some form of stigma awareness, although in no case was it frequent, and in most cases it was only expressed during the final phase of the study when their views were actively solicited by the researchers. Preoccupation with stratification issues within their current residential peer group was not evident, but all three participants did volunteer concern about stratification issues in other settings where there were heterogeneous client populations, e.g. their prior institutional experiences and an area-wide social club that they currently attended.

The participants affiliated with Agency D did not express a single concern related to stratification. During the conversation phase, four of the six participants affiliated with this agency did express awareness of their handicaps and recounted numerous stigmatic encounters with non-mentally handicapped people. Three of these four also denied that they were mentally retarded, as did most of the participants of the study. The other two of the six participants affiliated with Agency D did not reveal awareness or concern about stigma at any time. One of them, Wil, admitted that he was mentally retarded, and the other, Pete, said that he did not know. These two participants

---

*Level of functioning refers to such things as work status (day program, sheltered workshop, or job), degree of physical mobility, and communication skills.

did report a few encounters that appeared to be stigma-promoting, but they did not identify them as such, i.e. they revealed awareness of the inappropriateness of the behavior of the non-mentally handicapped people but did not associate it with their handicaps. It was not clear to the researcher whether this was a deliberate omission.

All but one of the participants affiliated with Agency D are black, and their parents are either working-class or poor. This agency, a group home, is located in a black, working-class, urban community. Seven different incidents were observed in which the neighbors in the immediate vicinity of the group home communicated in positive ways with the participants. Examples include a neighbor asking a participant to buy something for her at the grocery store, cordial verbal greetings on the street, a physical embrace, and an invitation to a neighbor's cookout. There were no comparable incidents observed at the other two group homes. The only recorded observations of this nature in other settings are two separate incidents in which neighbors were verbally cordial to participants affiliated with Agency B.

This variation in the findings could have been influenced by differences in what each researcher was attentive to, as the design of the study contained no systematic means for observing relations between participants and their neighbors. However, it appears that the participants residing at Agency D are more socially integrated into their neighborhood and that their lack of preoccupation with stigma issues may be associated with the feeling that they are more accepted by their neighbors. This finding is consistent with Henshel's (1972) findings, suggesting that the social networks within the black subculture are more accepting of mental retardation than those in the majority white culture.

In conclusion, the participants are aware — at times keenly aware — of their personal and social circumstances. This keenness is particularly evident in relation to their handicaps. The next chapter will describe numerous incidents in the lives of the participants. These incidents portray the participants' social intercourse with other clients, staff members, relatives, friends, acquaintances, and strangers and are intended to highlight some of the ways in which stigma is promoted.

Chapter 4

THE PROMOTION OF STIGMA

Mary: When visitors come into my [sheltered] workshop to see what is going on, they come up to me and say, 'What are you doing?' when it is obvious. I tell them, but I want to say 'What do you think I'm doing?'!

STIGMA is not inherent in a person's handicap. It originates with the values and norms of society and its countless subsystems, and it is transmitted by people, organizations, and institutions. Stigma is manifested when contact occurs between mentally handicapped people and those who transmit it. As Goffman (1963) put it, the encounters between the stigmatized and normals provide the primal scenes of sociology, as they reveal the causes and effects of stigma.

The term *stigma* is sometimes used by the public but tends to be only vaguely understood in terms of its origins and its effect on people with disabilities. Furthermore, the range of forms in which stigma is manifested is not readily known to most people. To the average person, stigma probably evokes singular images such as a cruel act committed against a defenseless disabled person or the violent reactions of alarmed residents attempting to stop disabled people from moving into their neighborhood.

In *Stigma*, Goffman (1963, p. 13) develops the concept of stigma. His concept encompasses three different types including the stigma associated with a minority race, nationality, or religion; the stigma deriving from deviant acts such as homosexuality or alcoholism; and the stigma associated with deformities of the body. He defines stigma as an attribute of a person that makes him both different from and less desirable than others in the category of persons available for him to be. The term *stigma*, however, applies more to the negative social meanings that are ascribed to the attribute than to the attribute itself.

One of the research questions in the study concerned how critical stigma is to the lives of the research participants. The author suspected that stigma pervaded their lives, and the study attempted to capture this pervasive quality, particularly as it was manifested in the participants' associations with other people.

In its three phases, the study created numerous and varied opportunities to observe and hear about incidents involving non-mentally handicapped people interacting with the participants. Many of these incidents involved inappropriate and demeaning communications with the participants because of their handicaps. More specifically, some of the incidents contained explicit negative references to a participant's handicap, and in others the association between the non-mentally retarded person's behavior and a participant's handicap was only suspected. Both these types of incidents were identified as "stigma-promoting." Thus, the definition of a stigma-promoting incident was any current incident* involving a non-mentally handicapped person and a participant in which the former either made an explicit depreciatory reference to a participant's handicap or communicated behavior toward a participant that was depreciatory and suspected by either the participant or researcher of being based on the participant's handicap.

---

*An incident was defined as current if it occurred during the period that the study was conducted or up to one year before the study began.

Fifty-five stigma-promoting incidents were identified in the study. Additional incidents were identified but not included in this presentation because they occurred prior to one year before the study began or there was a lack of evidence to substantiate that the incidents were "inappropriate." As an example of the latter case, six of the male participants reported that they had been fired from previous jobs, but it was not clear whether they were fired because of their inability to meet the demands of the job or for other reasons related to their handicaps.

Of the fifty-five incidents, forty-four were voluntarily reported by the participants. The researchers were not present when these incidents occurred. The other eleven incidents were observed by the researchers and determined to be stigma-promoting. The participants were not asked to confirm these observations. These fifty-five incidents involved twenty-two of the twenty-seven participants.

Forty of the fifty-five incidents involved staff members working within the mental retardation system. The staff worked in a wide range of settings including group homes, sheltered workshops, leisure programs, special night school classes, special tutorial programs, and counseling units of agencies. The remaining fourteen incidents involved employers, parents, neighbors, and strangers in public places. It should be noted that most of the researchers' observational time was spent at mental retardation settings and a much smaller portion of time was spent in other settings such as restaurants, shopping centers, or buses. Also, the participants typically spent most of their time within the mental retardation system. Therefore, it would be incorrect to conclude from this finding that staff members were more likely than others to interact inappropriately with the participants.

The study was not designed to measure how frequently stigma-promoting incidents occurred. The incidents presented here include only those that were either observed by the researchers or voluntarily shared by the participants. The primary value of this set of findings is in the descriptions of how stigma was promoted. Each of the fifty-five stigma-promoting incidents can be viewed as a unique portrayal of stigma promotion, involving a complex interplay of perceptions and behaviors by the parties.

The fifty-five incidents tend to cluster around thirteen themes. The themes are inappropriate language used in making references to a participant, inappropriate restrictions imposed on a participant, violations of confidentiality, deterring new roles, physical abuse, involuntary sterilization, excessively loud or scolding tone of voice, treating a participant in a childlike manner, imitation of the participant's limitations, denying opportunities for a participant to present his views, a pattern of ignoring a participant, open ridicule, and staring (See Table I).

INAPPROPRIATE LANGUAGE REFERENCES

Staff members, acquaintances, and strangers used inappropriate language in referring to the participants in eight instances, and in all eight cases these references were viewed as stigma promoting. The language used by strangers and acquaintances was usually harsh; they referred to the participants as "stupid," "Look, here comes the retardate," and "You look like a truck rolled over you." The particular references used by staff members seemed innocuous in intent, but the participants identified them as inappropriate and demeaning, e.g. "I got the pick of the litter" (referring to new clients discharged from an institution), and "You are a very capable little girl . . . I

TABLE I

STIGMA-PROMOTING INCIDENTS

Theme	No. of Incidents	Explicit/Implicit Reference to a Participant's Handicap	People Involved	Sources of Data	
				Participant	Researcher
1. Inappropriate language used in referring to a participant.	8	E	Strangers, acquaintances, staff	6	2
2. Inappropriate restrictions imposed on a participant.	9	I	Staff, board members	9	0
3. Violations of confidentiality	5	I	Staff	2	3
4. Deterring new roles	4	I	Staff	3	1
5. Physical abuse	4	I	Staff	4	0
6. Involuntary sterilization	1	I	Parent	1	0
7. Excessively loud or scolding tone of voice used	5	I	Staff	4	1

8. Being treated in a child-like manner	3	I	Staff, acquaintances	3	0
9. Imitation of a participants limitations	2	E/I	Staff	1	1
10. Denying a participant an opportunity to present his view	4	I	Staff	3	1
11. A pattern of ignoring a participant	2	I	Staff	2	0
12. Open ridicule	4	E/I	Strangers, acquaintances	3	1
13. Staring	4	E/I	Strangers	3	1
TOTAL	55			44	11

mean, grown woman."

INAPPROPRIATE RESTRICTIONS IMPOSED ON PARTICIPANTS

Nine incidents involved either inappropriate reasons for imposing restrictions or inappropriate forms of restrictions. Ron, for example, was told that he could not attend a dance sponsored by a club for mentally handicapped people because the staff thought that the club members were too low functioning. Ron wanted to attend because he was attracted to some of the women there. Another participant, Sol, felt it was inappropriate that the staff would not permit him to eat food in his bedroom.

Sometimes the language used to identify some of the restrictions seemed inappropriate. An "allowance" was withheld from one participant. Another participant was told "Go to your room" when he got into an argument with another client. Phillip was placed on "probation" at his agency for hitting another client. His response was, "I don't need this [probation]. It wasn't a big thing [hitting a client]. I can go to City Hall and see people who are really on probation."

Four of the incidents involved placing a blanket restriction on a group of clients without giving due consideration to individual differences. In one instance, all of the clients of Agency A, the multiservice agency, were prohibited from drinking alcoholic beverages at agency-sponsored events. Later this restriction was amended to include only those without the written consent of a doctor. Some of the participants resented this restriction because they drank alcoholic beverages in other settings and felt foolish drinking soda at the agency while other adults drank alcohol. In another incident, a number of clients were prohibited from using the cafeteria at a workshop during lunch periods even though some of them had not committed a misdeed. A third incident occurred during a vacation trip to another state; none of the clients was allowed to go out on his own at night even though some of them were quite capable of doing this. These participants resented being restricted because they were used to traveling freely at other times.

VIOLATIONS OF CONFIDENTIALITY

The confidentiality that professionals profess to uphold in regard to their clients' private lives was noticeably violated five times. One incident involved a staff member who told the researcher, without solicitation, that a participant had just begun having sexual relations with her boyfriend. Another incident involved two staff members who entertained each other during dinner with personal information about two participants. A third example involved a staff member who asked Paul a number of personal questions, stressing that his responses would be kept strictly confidential, and then discussed with Paul's parents some of the information that he shared.

DETERRING NEW ROLES

Inappropriate interaction was at times manifested by what people chose to ignore. In four situations, the participants verbalized a desire to be viewed differently than they had previously been. The most vivid case involved Eugene, who wanted to start a client committee to entertain severely disabled children in hospitals. Eugene explained, "I'm thankful I can see, hear, talk, cross my hands, and cross my legs. I'm thankful. That's why I want to help out other people." Eugene spent an entire year attempting to persuade the staff to help him, and he was still without staff support at the time that the study ended. Meanwhile, he held periodic meetings with other clients to keep his dream alive — and with it a new role for himself.

Another situation emerged in the client group led by a staff member and one of the researchers. Roger, a client in this group, announced after meeting with the group for three months that he would no longer attend to get help because he did not need the help of the group anymore. He said that he would continue coming to the group as an informal leader because he felt that he could help the other clients by sharing his own experiences with them. Unfortunately, the leaders did not actively support this participant's shifting role because his wishes were unusual and perhaps threatening as well.

A third situation occurred on an agency-sponsored trip to another state. Nancy and Roger chose to disassociate themselves from responsibility for Mary, who needed to be pushed around in her wheelchair. These two participants felt that they were on the trip to enjoy themselves and that spending large amounts of their time caring for Mary was diverting them from their fun. Also, these two participants seemed to want to disassociate themselves from the stigma symbols inherent in Mary's physical condition. The staff members were persistent in their efforts to enlist Nancy and Roger to do what they felt was their moral responsibility— taking care of their peer, and they berated these participants for their unwillingness to cooperate.

The fourth situation involved Ron, who was ill. In his words, "I was out of it. I just sat and wanted to watch TV. Then Mildred [a staff person] came in and yelled, 'What's wrong? What's wrong with your mind?' " Ron responded to the researcher, "I just wanted to be left alone, to be able to lie in bed, and when she [staff person] would come in to turn over and tell her, 'It's just not my day.'"

PHYSICAL ABUSE

In four instances, participants were physically abused by staff members. In one case, a participant had attempted to sexually seduce a younger boy, and the staff member's response was to teach the participant a lesson by giving him boxing gloves and challenging him to what became a brutal boxing match. The other three incidents involved staff members slapping or grabbing participants for disobeying a rule or otherwise committing an act that was unacceptable to the staff.

INVOLUNTARY STERILIZATION

This incident involved Jim, who discovered that he was having a vasectomy at the same time he was hospitalized for other surgery. He said that he did not know why his parents wanted him to have the vasectomy, but he reluctantly went along with it.

EXCESSIVELY LOUD OR SCOLDING TONE OF VOICE

Five participants reported being spoken to by staff members at such a high volume that it was quite apparent to them that the communication was inappropriate. One incident involved a vocational counselor, the researcher, and Hank. The researcher was encouraging Hank to explain what he does at the workshop. Instead of allowing Hank to do so, the counselor, speaking in a very loud voice, said, "You put bolts in a bag, don't you? . . . You seal bags . . . You put bags in boxes . . . " It was apparent to both Hank and the researcher that the counselor talked as if Hank were almost deaf and too stupid to speak for himself.

At times, staff members talked loudly to an entire client group when only some of the clients had hearing impairments. As Susan explained in one of these instances, "She [staff person] treats everyone alike. She hollers at everyone. Some should be talked to loudly, but not others. If she would not yell but be gentle, she would get more cooperation."

CHILDLIKE TREATMENT

In three incidents, people treated participants as if they were children. In one case, a friend of the family pinched Dora on the cheek. In another, a staff person patted Nancy on the head and shoulders and then talked to her "like a baby," according to Nancy. In another incident, a customer of Mary's father commented about Mary, "Isn't she nice?" Mary's response in private to her father was, "Would you get her out of here?"

IMITATION OF A PERSON'S LIMITATIONS

Two incidents involved staff members who imitated clients when the clients spoke or behaved in an unacceptable manner, e.g. when George slouched in his chair and Susan spoke with a high voice. In the first instance, George explained to the researcher that he did not think this was right. He added, "We have feelings like everyone else." In the second instance, a staff member amusingly imitated Susan's speech problem while talking about her.

DENYING A PARTICIPANT AN OPPORTUNITY
TO PRESENT HIS VIEW

One of the four instances of this type of stigma promotion involved Ron, who lived in a small group residence and was unexpectedly sent to another group home on a trial basis. He was extremely angry about this because the "big shots" sent him without even asking him what he wanted. Later, the same action recurred without his input. In another instance, Paul chose to withdraw from an agency activity because it reminded him of an earlier traumatic experience. Instead of asking Paul about this traumatic experience, the staff person called his sister for an explanation without informing him. Paul told the researcher that he did not object to the call, but he wanted the staff member to consult him first.

A PATTERN OF IGNORING A PARTICIPANT

In two instances, participants felt that they were being consistently ignored by a staff member when asking a question or making a request. In one instance, for example, John said to a staff member, "I want to speak to you." The staff member said it would have to wait until later. John repeated his request three more times, being very firm that he wanted to talk. The staff person also remained firm in ignoring him. Afterward, John explained, "She [staff member] doesn't understand me. If she did she would answer me . . . she is too busy with many things."

OPEN RIDICULE

Four incidents were identified in which participants were openly ridiculed. Three of these incidents involved strangers. In one instance a stranger sat down next to Helen on a public bus and then got up and sat elsewhere after she caught a glimpse of Helen's appearance. The comments that followed between Helen and Dora indicated that this was not an isolated occurrence. Helen said, "Did you see that lady move?" Dora replied, "Yeah, that's why I gave her that look. People do that to me all the time."

In another instance, Louise was riding on the subway, and two girls across the aisle were laughing. When they got off, they stopped laughing, confirming her suspicion that they were laughing at her. Doc, who has difficulty walking, explained his experiences this way, "Every time I go out on the street, people laugh at me. I guess it's something that I do that people don't want me to do."

STARING

Staring was another form of blatant disregard of the participants' feelings that was reported by some of them. Four participants indicated that they were keenly aware of it when it occurred. As Louise explained, "Sometimes when I am waiting for a bus, people stare at me." She said that she knew they were staring even if she was not looking at them. She said, "It's like you feel it, and you turn around, and they are looking at you." Mary said, "People stop and stare at me. It's okay with children. They don't know any better. But adults? It makes me angry. I feel like saying, "Take a picture, it lasts longer!"

SUMMARY

It is significant that in forty-four of the fifty-five stigma-promoting incidents the participants viewed the others' reactions as depreciating of them and motivated by the others' awareness of their handicap. The study was not designed to elicit the stigma promoters' perceptions of the incidents, and it seems likely that in many instances their perceptions of what happened may have been substantially different and their actions may at times have even been based on professional grounds. Nevertheless, the participants' perceptions of the incidents should not be minimized even when they revealed only a partial or even distorted account of what happened. It should be noted that the researchers observed incidents of stigma promotion representing eight of the thirteen types identified, partially substantiating the perceptions of the participants.

The people involved as stigma promoters varied by type of incident. Some types of incidents involved people who had no knowledge of or relationship with the participants. These incidents often contained behaviors that were openly harsh and grossly insensitive. Other types of incidents involved people who were familiar with the participants and their handicaps and maintained ongoing relationships with them. These incidents, with some exceptions, tended to reveal more subtle forms of depreciatory communication and tended to be more difficult to verify because they were part of ongoing relationships with prescribed statuses and roles.

Most of the stigma-promoting incidents contained only implicit references to the participants' handicaps. Yet, in most of these cases, the participants keenly sensed that the stigma promoters were motivated by their awareness of the participants' handicaps. Nine of the fourteen types of incidents or themes contained only an implicit rather than explicit reference. Among these types, some (e.g. Table I: 2, 6, 7, 8, 11) tend to be problems more peculiar to people with physical and mental disabilities, while others (e.g. Table I:3,4,10) may be more universal to any client population within the human service system. In both sets of cases, the incidents are considered stigma promoting, with the underlying assumption being that problems faced by people with mental handicaps may also be faced by other groups of people in similar social circumstances.

The next chapter focuses on the participants' patterns of response to the various forms of stigma in their lives. Specific questions to be explored are How do the participants feel about stigma promotion? Should they exploit their stigmatic status or hide it? Should they associate with people and programs that are identified for the mentally retarded? If not, what are their alternatives and how realistic are they?

Chapter 5

RESPONDING TO STIGMA

Phillip: When are you guys going to wise up? You got to know what you're doing. You wouldn't treat yourselves that way.

PEOPLE with mental handicaps often are viewed as helpless victims of their social circumstances. Even though recognition is given to the often adverse and demeaning conditions that these people are exposed to, not enough consideration is given to equipping them with the means of protecting and maintaining themselves in the community. Possibly they are not thought to be capable of confronting another person's prejudice or managing themselves when faced with ridicule, or perhaps a prevalent view is that the burden of defending themselves is too much to expect considering the heavy burden that they already carry. Whatever the reasons for this inaction, the effects are the same: encouraging people with mental handicaps to be helpless.

When the heterogeneity within the population that is labeled mentally retarded is considered, including the wide variation in the nature of their handicaps and life experiences, it becomes obvious that the view of them as helpless is a stereotype that should be challenged. If it is recognized that many people with mental handicaps are aware of the stigma in their lives, an important question needs to be asked: "How do they cope with stigma?" This question was explored in the study and is the topic of this chapter.

Within the limits of the study's design, the researchers attempted to identify and examine the reactions and responses of the participants to the stigma that they encountered. Five categories of responses to stigma were identified. The first category characterizes the participants in a beginning phase of learning how to cope with stigma while the other categories identify options taken by the participants as they become more proficient in their efforts to cope with and manage stigma. This presentation is not meant to be an exhaustive coverage of all possible options in the management of stigma. Rather, it should be viewed as a beginning exploration of several patterns of responses that were observed. Some of the categories were generated from the data of the study while others were based on theoretical concepts (e.g. passing) that were supported by data in the study.

BEGINNING TO COPE WITH STIGMA

Encounters with stigma often cause anguish for the participants. A depreciating remark, cold stare, or willful disregard of a person's viewpoint hurts some of them in unimaginable ways. The pain derives not only from each stigma-promoting incident but also from the cumulative effect of numerous previous incidents, with the latest one serving as a further reminder of their inferior status.

Many of the participants were asked how they felt about their encounters with stigma. The most frequent type of response was that they wished to avoid talking about it or to minimize its importance. The bus scene mentioned in Chapter 4, in which a passenger sat next to Helen, noticed her, and then moved to sit somewhere else, resulted in Helen's expressing awareness of what had happened, and the way that she chose to handle it was to get off the bus and walk the rest of the way home alone.

Many of the participants, when asked how they felt about such encounters, said something like, "I don't want to think about it," "I don't let it upset me," or "I don't want to talk about it." Yet it was evident, in most of these cases, that the experiences were painful for the participants; the pain simply was difficult to express.

Paul revealed both the intensity of his feelings and the passivity of his response. He said that a stigma-promoting incident with a staff person upset him so much that he could not work well at his job for an entire week. Nevertheless, he chose not to tell the staff person how he felt. Helen, when asked how she felt about being called mentally retarded, expressed her pain by saying, "I feel invisible . . . half down. I feel like nothing. I have been called dumb and crazy and on these occasions I sometimes get angry and tell people to get away . . . or I just walk away."

Overall, this category of response to stigma is characterized as a tendency to be without a conscious approach to or consistent pattern of dealing with stigma. The participants with this tendency seem to realize and feel the discomfort of stigma, but they lack sophistication in knowing what to do about it. Their reactions to it are usually not premeditated; instead they represent a set of haphazard responses to the stigma that is encountered.

This tendency to be unprepared and in some ways defenseless is suspected of being associated with how well the participants understand the nature and origins of their stigma-related problems. The participants with this tendency are not sure whether to blame themselves or the other person if a stigma-promoting incident occurs. Doc, who has cerebral palsy that restricts his mobility, revealed his confusion when he said, "Every time I go out on the street people laugh at me. I guess it's something that I do that people don't want me to do. I don't walk straight. I can't walk straight." He added, "A strange feeling comes over me when I walk. You think you're no good, that you will step on people's toes."

The confusion about who is responsible for their stigma-related problems derives from the confusion that the participants have about their identities. The question of whether they perceive themselves as mentally retarded is a case in point. As the findings in Chapter 3 reveal, most of the participants denied that they were mentally retarded, but eight expressed confusion or stated that they did not know. As Jill put it, "In some ways I'm retarded and in some ways I'm not. I'm afraid of people and don't like to get close. I'm afraid I will get treated as I did as a child." To Jill, being mistreated is associated with an earlier time in her life when she was considered mentally retarded. As an adult she is still influenced by her childhood experiences, but she is also beginning to question her earlier identity.

A shifting identity characterizes many of the participants. As children they may have passively accepted the mental retardation label and their status as a mentally retarded child, but as adults who live in the community and assume increasing responsibility for themselves their self-perceptions are changing. To varying degrees they feel ambivalent about their handicap status because they are developing increasing conviction that they are more normal than handicapped. However, this shift in their identity does not seem to be a consistent move forward; their feelings and perceptions tend to vacillate between these two conflicting identities. Many factors thwart their movement toward a more normal identity, including their internal tapes from the past that periodically resurface, the confusions that their parents, staff, and others convey about their identities, and their continued encounters with stigma promotion in all aspects of their lives.

This state of ambivalence about their identities is clearly a developmental one. As they become increasingly responsible for themselves personally, economically, and socially, they are also gaining increasing conviction that they are more normal than handicapped. Furthermore, as they reexamine the questions of who they are and whether they still consider themselves mentally retarded, they are gaining perspective on the stigma in their lives.

Four additional patterns of response to stigma were identified. Two of these patterns, seeking the secondary benefits of being mentally retarded and resisting stigma, were observed in social situations where their identities were known. The third pattern, passing, was observed in situations where their identities were not known, and the fourth pattern, covering, was manifested in both types of settings.

SEEKING THE SECONDARY BENEFITS

One tendency that people with mental handicaps have is to allow stigma promotion to happen and even to actively invite it to occur if benefits are available. Lemert (1972) identifies this tendency as promoting "the positive side of a negative identity." Lemert believes that the stigma associated with a deviant identity is not likely to be contained, particularly for those who deviate significantly from society's norms. The alternative is to enlist efforts that will make the most of a deviant situation. Stigma promotion thus becomes a solution for some, as it contains benefits for being mentally retarded.

One stereotyped image of people with mental handicaps encourages this tendency. This image characterizes these people as objects of pity (Wolfensberger, 1976). The retarded person is perceived as a victim of a condition for which he is not responsible and which he can do little to overcome. There is interest in bringing happiness to him but without any serious intent to develop capabilities that will make him more independent.

This image takes visual form when a mentally handicapped person ventures out into the community. The handicapped attributes of the person elicit sympathy from some of the people whom he meets in public places. Such people wish to do something, however small, to "help," setting in motion an exchange that is likely to promote the positive side of a negative identity. An incident involving Ann illustrates this. Ann, a petite woman who at times projects a sweet, dependent image, manipulated her circumstances one evening while waiting in the rain with her peers for a bus. She and her two friends were beginning to get soaked because they had forgotten their umbrellas. A woman appeared, and before long Ann was invited to join the woman under her umbrella. The woman protectively placed her arm around her and upon boarding the bus invited Ann to sit by her. Meanwhile, Ann's two friends sat several seats behind them and mused about her shrewdness.

Similarly, behaving as a docile, dependent client in an agency may bring the secondary benefits of special attention from a staff member. Ron shared his understanding of what happens when he behaves in this way at his agency. He said that by being "nice" he is called "honey bunch," "sweetie pie," and "handsome" by the staff. He feels ambivalent about his circumstances, however, as he added: "Be nice and you'll get a lollipop or ice cream . . . That's when I was a child . . . Now I am a man."

The mental retardation system in general has a tendency to promote the positive side of the clients' negative identity. Client status in this system provides people with many services and opportunities that would otherwise be denied them. One opportunity that the system provides is a social context for clients to meet and develop relationships with other clients. Friendships, romantic relationships, and explorations of common interest all become possible when a person becomes a client of the system. Without this system, virtually none of these associations would develop. John, for example, who works at a sheltered workshop, has developed a long-term romantic relationship with a young woman who also works there. In the past John was able to visit his woman friend at her family's home, but her father decided to stop these visits. This action left John with only one place to see her — at the workshop. He takes advantage of every opportunity available to him to be with his friend, including coffee breaks, lunch, and immediately before and after workshop hours. He privately admits that the sole reason he wants to be a client of the workshop is to be with her, and he is determined not to leave and take an outside job because it would mean leaving her. John's circumstances suggest that the mental retardation system is needed not only to develop these associations but to maintain them as well.

Another special benefit of the mental retardation system is the access that the clients have to a group of typically attractive, sensitive, and caring people — the staff members. Perhaps there is nothing more ego-deflating than to be ignored or shunned when approaching another employee at the work site or a potential date at a social event. People who are employed by the mental retardation system are expected not to ignore or shun their clients. Respect, sensitivity, and interest are expectations of their work roles, which often foster the development of associations between staff members and clients.

When asked to identify their closest friends, many of the participants mentioned favorite current or former staff members. In almost all of these cases, the staff member probably would not concur that the relationship is a genuine friendship, but the fact that these relationships, however nonintimate, exist is most significant to the participants. A physically attractive female staff member with an equally vibrant personality provides an illustration of this point. She is the program director of one of the affiliate agencies and the most popular staff member of the agency. It is not uncommon for her to have a trail of clients following her wherever she goes, and many of the male clients in particular share fantasies of being her lover, husband, or friend outside the agency. Undoubtedly these clients would not have the benefit of this association if she were not a staff member.

The programs can also be perceived as reinforcing the positive side of a negative identity at times, as they convey the message that being mentally retarded means having access to special programs that are unavailable to other people. The three affiliate agencies that provide group homes and apartment living arrangements are examples. They provide well-furnished, government-financed living units, and the primary eligibility requirement is that the occupant be mentally retarded. Karen expressed understanding of this secondary gain when an apartment became available to her. She had lived her entire life with her mother, and at the age of 28 she wanted more freedom to date and assert her independence. As she explained it, "I would still be living at home if it hadn't been for being mentally retarded."

Another example of a special program is the vacation

clubs that offer trips for handicapped people to faraway places like Israel, England, and Hawaii. Previous to the emergence of these clubs, some of the participants had not traveled outside their county without being accompanied by their parents. Now some of them are traveling abroad with supervisory staff, staying at first-class hotels, eating at fine restaurants, and visiting popular tourist sights. All this is possible because they qualify as handicapped clients.

Promoting the positive side of a negative identity is not necessarily harmful. The mental retardation system clearly meets many basic needs of its clients, and probably most of these needs would be ignored if there were no such system available. However, while in most instances the benefits provided by the system seem to promote the development and normalization of the client population, in some instances these benefits have a contrary effect. More attention should be given to understanding how the benefits of the mental retardation system discourage clients from becoming more independent and leaving the system when its services are no longer needed.

RESISTING STIGMA

Another option available to people with mental handicaps is to resist the stigma that they encounter. A prevalent view held by the public is that the advocacy role is beyond the capabilities of these people; others are needed to do it for them. This view has been internalized by handicapped people as well. Their socialization has convinced them that their views must be represented by other people while they are expected to remain acquiescent, cooperative, and grateful for what they have.

An opposing view is that people with mental handicaps do have the potential, if not a developing capacity, to be their own agents of change. While relatively few people with mental handicaps may gravitate toward this tendency, those who do deserve closer examination.

Most of the participants seem reluctant to speak out when their needs are disregarded or minimized. Because of the advantages that they have, they are hesitant to challenge people in authority, particularly parents and staff persons who supervise aspects of their lives. However, some of the participants are critical of their circumstances and at times seem ready to take steps to improve them. As Eugene told the researcher, "I'm different than I was when I was new at [the agency] fifteen years ago. I'm more outspoken now, and probably most people don't like it."

Some of the comments and actions of the participants reveal their intentions to resist what they perceive as stigma promoting. A few of the participants affiliated with Agency A were actively confronting their affiliate agency for inappropriately using the mental retardation label when referring to the clients of the agency in a fund-raising drive. They do not perceive the label to be an accurate description of most of the clients, and they are persistent in demanding its discontinuance.

Karen wrote a letter to the director of the hospital where she is employed to complain about the way that some staff members interact with other staff members, like her, who are handicapped. In her letter she stated that she wondered how they would be able to deal with all the different types of people whom they serve if they did not develop more sensitivity for those with whom they work. She was still waiting for a reply to her letter when the study ended approximately eight months after she had sent it.

Another form of resistance to stigma promotion is to pursue new, largely unexplored roles, particularly within familiar social settings. In Chapter 4, illustrations were given of new roles that participants wished to assume.

Change often is sought when a person feels that he has been treated unjustly. Anger serves as the underlying catalyst for seeking redress. People with mental handicaps are not often thought to be comfortable expressing anger, yet some of the participants expressed anger when they encountered stigma. Sometimes this anger is expressed as a defiant act such as laughing at or deliberately ignoring an order issued by a staff person. Occasionally anger is expressed openly in the form of rage. Some of the participants expressed their anger periodically to the researchers, once they realized that it would not lead to negative consequences such as a reprimand or suspension from a program. Ron talked angrily about "the big shots" when describing how he was denied input into the decision to transfer him to another residence. Phillip aired his feelings with the researcher after knowing him for about a year. He was referring to the staff of his agency when he said, "When are you guys going to wise up? You got to know what you're doing. You wouldn't treat yourselves that way." Such expressions of anger are not regular occurrences for the participants, but they are significant, and they can be viewed as an important step toward taking more control over their lives.

PASSING

According to Goffman (1963), many stigmatized people discover at some time in their lives that they can pass as someone with a less stigmatic identity or as a normal person. While passing may not be an option for mentally handicapped people who have obtrusive stigmatic attributes that are unalterable, it is a potential option for many others.

The inclination to develop proficiency in passing may be strong because of the advantages that can accrue from being perceived as normal or less stigmatic. Passing may first be experienced unwittingly, without the person realizing that it is occurring. The next stage may involve the person's discovering that he is passing while it is occurring. From there, a person may pass for fun or nonroutine activities. Finally, a person may develop a capability to pass during regular activities at work, in his neighborhood, and while using public services (Goffman, 1963, p. 79).

Passing was almost never mentioned by the participants, but it was occasionally observed. Some of the manifestations seemed to involve insignificant activities. For example, Sol was observed purchasing a newspaper and carrying it home on the bus even though he cannot read. Apparently he was attempting to portray himself as a normal bus passenger reading a newspaper.

Eugene usually chooses not to count his change when making a purchase at a store because the excessive time that he would need would give him away. He admitted to doing this when he said, "I have to train myself to get the change. I can figure it out but it takes me a couple of seconds longer. I know how to count but to make sure I get the right change [is difficult] . . . I should check it more closely than I do sometimes. I just take the change and that's it . . . I guess whatever a person wants to do they can do."

Sometimes passing involves concealing associations with other people who have stigmatic attributes. An interesting example of this took place on an agency-sponsored trip to a baseball game. Two participants who are not noticeably handicapped chose independently of each other to disassociate themselves from the other clients by walking a short distance behind them on the way to the game and by leaving alone just before the game ended.

In some instances, passing was observed to be more vital to the participants' basic needs. Janet, being acutely aware that the group home where she lives could be viewed as a giveaway of her status, decided to tell her male visitors that the home was a place where people pay board. Five participants who had previously been institutionalized attempted to hide their status when asked by the researcher why they had been there. Their explanations, which follow, reflected a problem much less severe than mental retardation:

> Sol: I was there to help out the others. That's what the staff told me.
>
> John: My behavior was backward.
>
> Scott: I was there for two reasons. My mother didn't have the money to take care of me and I got caught stealing with my cousin.
>
> Doc: The school I went to was torn down and my mother couldn't take care of me anymore because she had four jobs so I went to [the institution].
>
> George: I was fighting all the time. I first went to X Hospital because I had seizures and had to take medication. Then I went to [the institution].

These five participants were denying their mental retardation status and the inappropriateness of their affiliation with an institution for the mentally retarded. As presented earlier, most of the participants denied perceiving themselves as mentally retarded, and one of the motives for these responses may have been a need to pass as someone with a less stigmatic identity.

Roger revealed the anxiety that can be involved in attempting to pass when he said, "At a place with other people, you have to . . . they go around and each says something. One says he is in college, taking psychology. Another is a speech therapist. The next one says she is a teacher, and when it gets to me, I say I graduated from high school and work for the government as a clerk. It [the job] doesn't knock you down . . . builds you up. A guy that sweeps floors, it doesn't do anything for you. Here I have a skill, work in an office. Before I worked at refinishing furniture at Goodwill Industries. I'd say I refinish furniture at Good*man* Industries or something else. I had to lie . . . which isn't good, but now I don't have to."

Goffman (1963) describes the final phase of passing as one in which passing occurs in all aspects of one's life, with the secret being known only to the passer himself and possibly to a few additional people who assist him in his concealment. In this phase a person who has been labeled mentally retarded and has lived in the mentally retarded world would be prepared to leave it to live in the normal world.

While most of the participants are noticeably discontented with life in their confined world, only five were observed to be ready to leave it. Four of them (Nancy, Roger, Karen, and Janet) have an active client status with their affiliate agencies, while one (Noreen) currently has an inactive status. A closer examination of these five participants sheds some light on the nature of this transitionary phase.

Three overall characteristics seem to capture the circumstances of these participants. First, the keen awareness of their stigmatic circumstances that almost all of the participants reveal seems intensified for these five participants. They tend to feel and express more discomfort with their circumstances, and they seem particularly preoccupied with stratification issues. Regarding the latter, they often go out of their way to inform others that they are superior to and fundamentally different from their lower functioning peers. In addition, they have a greater tendency than the other participants to avoid contacts with lower functioning peers, particularly in public places. This tendency apparently reflects an intensified alienation to their stigmatic status, with these peers being a painful reminder of it.

Second, these five participants are more involved in the non-mentally retarded world than the other participants. All five hold jobs on the outside and more often frequent discos and bars for entertainment. They also associate with non-mentally handicapped people more than the other participants. Of the six participants mentioned in Chapter 2 who identified non-mentally handicapped people as friends, four are among these five participants in transition. These participants seem to be able to establish such relationships with more success. Noreen has had the most success with developing outside relationships and has already discontinued her friendships with clients within her affiliate agency. She has done this by deciding not to return to this agency where these friendships originated and were maintained.

The third characteristic that captures the circumstances of these five participants is that they appear and behave more normal than the others. They are not necessarily more intelligent. Essentially, their stigma symbols are less evident and thus they can pass more easily in public.

The metaphor of two separate worlds developed in Chapter 2 conveys the profound sense of separation that seems to exist between the participants' world and the normal world. In a sense, a wall exists between these worlds, as the participants cannot move freely back and forth. If the wall has a portal, it is not one that is accessible for frequent movement between the two worlds but a one-way exit to the non-mentally retarded world. If the participants can get out, they realize that they have to stay out, i.e. disassociate themselves from the world left behind.

For these five participants, there appears to be no established portal to normal living. Although society has developed methods for labeling them and socializing them into a mentally retarded world, the methods for delabeling them and disengaging them from this world are almost nonexistent. Noreen, who has already left her affiliate agency, worked out her exit by building a support system in the normal world and then, upon succeeding, simply abandoning the mentally retarded world. The move from a group home to an apartment was intended as part of an exit plan by Karen, who realized that she could become much more independent of the mental retardation system and staff by living in an apartment. The system is supporting this plan without fully realizing why it is so important to her. Janet was planning an escape exit during the time of the study by secretively planning to marry a man who is living independently.

These findings on passing are somewhat different from Edgerton's (1967) findings. Edgerton concluded that passing was critical for his subjects' survival. This study's lack of evidence that passing was critical and frequently practiced by the participants' may have been due to the nature of the settings that were observed. Most of the research observations were conducted in settings where the participants mental retardation status was known, whereas passing would most likely occur in places where their status was unknown. Also, passing may have been rarely reported by the participants because it would seem to be inextricably and subconsciously linked to their self-concept, which was not a topic for open discussion. Passing and denial were evident, as they were in Edgerton's study, when inquiries were made pertaining to the participants' previous residence in a mental institution. As indicated earlier in this chapter, some of the participants who had resided in mental institutions denied that they were there because they were mentally retarded. All of Edgerton's subjects had been recent residents of a mental institution, and their denial of mental retardation status appeared to be closely linked to a need to disassociate themselves from the institution. A follow-up study ten years later revealed that Edgerton's subjects were then less concerned with stigma and passing, and this may have been the result of the time elapsed since their institutionalization (Edgerton and Bercovici, 1976).

Edgerton also stated that his subjects tended to divide their world into the few people who had explicit knowledge of their status and assisted them in passing and the many who knew nothing. The few who knew their status were called "benefactors" and included landlords, spouses, employers, and others. In contrast, only a few of the participants in this study reported that they were dependent on benefactors or collaborators. The participants' environment, unlike that of the subjects in Edgerton's study, is designed to include people with collaborative roles. The small group residences and day programs within the mental retardation system are staffed with professionally trained and experienced people; also, some of the participants live with their parents. All of these people serve as collaborators to the participants, often in significant ways, but the participants have not had to invest a significant amount of energy in finding and maintaining these relationships as the subjects did in Edgerton's study. Thus the participants' survival does not appear to be critically linked to the need for collaborators because the preexistence of collaborators conceals their significance.

COVERING

The final option, covering, refers to instances when a person is willing to admit that he possesses a stigmatic attribute but attempts to keep the stigma from looming large (Goffman, 1963). The stigmatized person's objective is to divert attention away from his stigmatic attribute so that more normal interaction can occur.

Covering can be employed in social situations where a person's stigmatic identity is either known or not. It is different from passing in that the person is willing to admit possession of his stigmatic attribute; this is often by necessity because his identity is already known or his stigmatic attribute is immediately apparent. However, covering could be viewed as a special form of passing in situations where the person's identity is not known, as willingness to admit to the possession of a stigmatic attribute does not necessarily mean openly volunteering this information.

Covering is an option that is widely supported within mental retardation systems. Normalization philosophy argues that people with mental handicaps should appear and behave as normal as possible if they are to be positively received in the community (Wolfensberger, 1972).

Staff members who follow normalization principles often place emphasis on helping their clients to do such things as dress appropriately, follow good grooming practices, develop social skills, and respect the established norms of a neighborhood. Normalization principles also guide planners and administrators in the design and location of programs in the community.

Covering was observed in many different instances in the study. It was revealed in the fashionable clothing worn by most of the participants and in the latest hair styles worn by many of the women. It was often manifested as a primary objective of programming. Workshops were observed that taught skills on banking, shopping, use of public transportation, and other routine aspects of living. At Agency B, staff members were observed teaching the female residents how to use makeup. Agency A offered regular rap sessions on the social skills needed to meet and date people. This agency also offered disco dancing classes to prepare clients with the latest dance step in case they decided to venture out to a dance club or bar.

Most of the instances of covering that were observed involved the active support of staff members and parents whose intentions were to expand the recipients' repertoire of skills and enhance their attractiveness. The participants seemed to partake freely in these activities, and generally they seemed in favor of their objectives. However, they seldom shared with the researchers instances in which they were deliberately covering. Like the act of passing, covering may have been too intricately linked to their identities to be openly discussed. They may also have viewed it as a part of their maturation into adulthood rather than as a means of minimizing their stigma.

Covering was seldom discussed and also difficult to observe. It is difficult to identify an act of covering without having previous knowledge of a person's attribute when it was more obtrusive. Because the researchers had no prior acquaintance with the participants, covering was difficult to identify.

In summary, the variety of ways in which the participants respond to stigma reveals that they are playing a role in managing this problem. Many of the participants seem relatively unsophisticated and limited in the range of options that they exercise, but some participants reveal shrewdness and competency in the management of stigma in their lives. The next chapter provides several recommendations for facilitating and enhancing a mentally handicapped person's skills in stigma management.

Chapter 6

TO EMPOWER

Researcher: *What advice would you give people on the outside if you were asked?*

Jill: *Try to understand rather than walking away. People are people. Listen to them. It sounds dumb, doesn't it?*

Researcher: *No.*

A S the findings of the study reveal, the problem of stigma is a frequent preoccupation and a disturbing intrusion in the lives of the twenty-seven participants. For many of them, it is perhaps as overwhelming as their physical and intellectual limitations.

The participants' handicaps to varying degrees do impose limitations on their intellect, mobility, and social functioning, but these limitations have been a major focus of considerable previous research. Thus they have been intentionally de-emphasized in this study, which attempted to isolate and focus on the problem area of stigma.

People typically view stigma problems and the limitations inherent in a handicap as if they are aspects of the same problem, for they both revolve around the person with the handicap. The problems amenable to a medical explanation somehow are intermixed with the sociological ones. A danger in this tendency is that the problem area of stigma has been overlooked and neglected in research and practice.

As was stated in Chapter 1, the problems inherent in a bio-psychological handicap are fundamentally different from the stigma problems associated with it. The latter is a social phenomenon that is understood from particular sociological and anthropological perspectives. As Lemert (1972) points out, it is essentially a moral problem perpetuated primarily by society.

The findings in Chapter 4 provide a wide array of descriptions of how stigma was promoted; thirteen different categories were identified from the data. It is presumed that this typology is not an exhaustive one, as additional categories could be added. However, the findings on stigma promotion reveal that strangers, employers, family members, neighbors, staff members, and others were all involved as stigma promoters, as well as neighborhood groups, social agencies, businesses and other organizations.

The majority of the stigma-promoting incidents involved the staff of the mental retardation system. Since most of the participants' time and the researchers' observational time was spent within this system, it would be incorrect to conclude that people working for this system are more prone than others to promote stigma. However, the reality is that the system which has been established to serve people with mental handicaps also plays a primary role in promoting stigma, and this should be a matter of grave concern. Staff members tend to be the people most intimately involved with the clients of this system, and thus they probably have the greatest impact on their lives.

Richardson (1975, p. 87) states that everyone has been socialized at an early age to respond with anxiety, inhibitions, and aversion to people who violate their norms pertaining to appearance, behavior, and movement; people with mental handicaps tend to violate these norms. The staff members of the mental retardation system are usually attracted to their work by a genuine concern for their clients and a desire to make their lives more productive and happy, yet staff members, like others, are products of our society's socialization, which inculcates myths, misconceptions, and other biases about mental retardation and physical disabilities.

This suggests that a high priority should be given to establishing for staff members and volunteers training programs that will expose and confront these ill-conceived cognitive and affective notions and offer alternative notions that will promote the clients' development. Staff and volunteers should be helped to examine themselves — their insensitivities, misconceptions, stereotypes, and stigma-promoting practices; they should also be helped to explore and analyze the origins of these problems in their socialization processes, agency policies, and other current and historical social forces.

These in-service training programs can provide useful data for designing training programs in the community, as the attitudinal barriers of the general public may be more clearly understood vis-à-vis the attitudinal barriers of service delivery personnel.

Beyond the mental retardation system, the social systems that touch the lives of people with mental handicaps are numerous and virtually beyond the reach of a community education program; therefore, the systems having the most contact and influence should be the other primary targets for a community education drive. High priority should be given to the neighborhoods where people with mental handicaps live, including not only their immediate neighbors but also local civic and political organizations, businesses, churches, clubs, and other significant units in the neighborhood.

Priority should also be given to reaching the teaching personnel and students in the school systems, beginning at the earliest levels. The schools are recognized as a major source of early socialization and should be helped to become centers for transmitting positive and accurate information and attitudes about mental disabilities.

Finally, high priority should be given to the generic agencies that have an actual or potential impact on the lives of people with mental handicaps. Employment training programs, YMCA/YWCAs and recreation centers, family planning agencies, health clinics, mental health centers, and marriage clinics are among the generic agencies that can be utilized by people with mental handicaps and should be equipped to effectively serve them.

THE SYMBOLS OF STIGMA

The general public often has incorrect perceptions of people with mental handicaps. This tendency is most evident in the comments made by residents opposing mentally handicapped people as neighbors. People typically cannot see beyond a person's handicap. In their minds, the handicap carries such significance that it overshadows the person and other aspects of his identity.

The characteristics of a person's handicap that evoke negative reactions in others begin the exchange of stigma promotion. These most noticeable aspects of a person's handicap serve as identifiers of his stigma. Clearly, more attention needs to be given to the stigma symbols that evoke strong negative reactions in others, for possibly they are as important in predicting successful community adjustment as IQ and adaptive behavior scores.

The stigma symbols of people with mental handicaps can derive from a range of physical, intellectual, and behavioral abnormalities. They can be, for example, limited verbal skills, immature behavior, inappropriate responses to questions, volatile fits of anger, inappropriate hugging, drooling, clumsiness, characteristics of Down's syndrome, abnormal body proportions, a speech impediment, etc. Further examples of personal stigma symbols are presented in Chapter 2 as some of the participants'.

In addition to these personal symbols, cues that are external to the person also can be identifiers of stigma. Particular associations and organizational affiliations are the most noticeable symbols of this type in the study's findings. Associating with other disabled people who have more severe stigmatic attributes can become a stigma identifier largely because it draws more attention to a person's own stigmatic attributes. Affiliations with particular groups, programs, organizations, and buildings also can be identifiers of stigma. Being in the company of twenty disabled people on a subway, for example, is an obvious stigma identifier. Appearing at a social club for handicapped people, living in a group home, and riding in an agency-identified van are other examples.

A wide array of stigma symbols evoke negative reactions in others and should become a more focused concern in combatting stigma. A concerted effort should continue to be made to eliminate or reduce personal identifiers that are easily amenable to change, such as inappropriate clothing and personal grooming, and a more ambitious commitment is needed in efforts to modify attributes that are more difficult to change, such as undeveloped social skills and limited motor coordination. Even stigma identifiers that initially appear to be unalterable may be amenable to change, such as the physical characteristics of Down's syndrome, which may be concealed through surgery (Sandahl, 1978).

Stigma symbols that derive from particular associations and agency affiliations may be among the easiest identifiers to be changed and therefore should be a primary target in reducing stigma. Agency policies and programs should be thoroughly scrutinized to discern whether they contain identifiers of stigma. Examples of questions that could be asked are the following:

Are clients unnecessarily traveling in large groups when they are in public places?

Are higher functioning people arbitrarily grouped with lower functioning people without considering the effect of this grouping on the former?

Do clients primarily attend social functions that are attended only by handicapped people?

Do they utilize the services of generic agencies and organizations when they are available or do they rely strictly on the services of the mental retardation system?

When using generic agencies, do clients utilize them individually or in conspicuously large groups?

Does the agency unnecessarily advertise the mental retardation label or other identifiers of stigma on its motor vehicles, buildings, and letterheads?

Does the staff unnecessarily share information with others about their clients' disability, level of functioning, and general status?

Other examples of stigma identifiers of this nature are

presented in *PASS 3* (1975), a field manual designed for evaluating human service agencies.

The mental retardation label is another symbol of stigma, maybe the most harmful one of all. Most of the participants in the study denied that they were mentally retarded, even though most of the people who know them perceive them by this label. Other studies concur with these findings that people whose IQs fall within a mild or moderate range of retardation usually perceive their handicaps as a specific, localized condition, such as a learning deficit or a physical disability, and deny being mentally retarded (Edgerton, 1967; Lorber, 1974; Braginsky and Braginsky, 1971; Heshusius, 1981; Gan, Tymchuk, and Nishihara, 1977). It is suspected that a relatively high percentage of people who are labeled mentally retarded do not identify themselves by this label.

One of the reasons that people who are labeled mentally retarded sometimes give for disavowing the label is important in understanding their position. They view mental retardation as a generalized debilitation in which a person is incapable of taking care of himself or making his own decisions. This definition, which may be commonly held by the general public, more accurately characterizes people with severe and profound levels of retardation rather than mild and moderate levels.

People's perceptions of someone who is identified by this label undoubtedly are colored by their own attitudes toward mental retardation. Even people who have an accurate definition must consciously resist the tendency to expect or think less of people identified by this label.

A less pejorative label certainly would be helpful to the labeled, and perhaps people who are labeled mildly and moderately retarded could be distinguished from the severely and profoundly retarded. In fact, in most cases these two groups have different etiologies for their conditions, with the former group more likely having an environmental, familial, or unknown cause and the latter more likely having an organic diagnosis (Kurtz, 1977, pp. 46-48).

However, merely changing the label will not be a panacea if nothing else changes. A new label must be accompanied by fundamental changes in the ways that we relate to those who are labeled. For while a new label may appear to lessen the impact of stigma, it may also take on a pejorative connotation in time, as has happened in the past, e.g. the use of moron, idiot, and imbecile.

TO BE CENTRAL PARTICIPANTS

The participants in this study are aware of their stigmatic attributes. They reveal a keen sensitivity to the cues or identifiers that evoke special attention in others, and in some instances they attempt to manipulate these identifiers to their favor either by minimizing or concealing them or by tolerating them to gain secondary benefits. In short, they are actors in the dramas that involve them.

A major tenet in the prescription for combatting stigma in this text is that people with mental handicaps should have the opportunity to become central participants in the battle. The illusion that they can be protected and sheltered from the harsh realities of stigma should no longer be promoted. In fact, they have the most at stake in changing the stigma-promoting conditions. Granted, many people will not have the capacity or inclination to get involved, but the decision about their participation should be made on an individual basis and involve their input.

To participate in stigma management and resistance, people with mental handicaps must be able to talk freely about themselves, their handicaps, and their stigma problems. An atmosphere needs to be created and nurtured in which questions, feelings, and views can be openly expressed. While individual discussions with staff, family members, and others may be useful in this, group sessions with other handicapped people may have the greatest impact. Peer group sessions can provide opportunities for people to share and learn from each other. It seems significant that the participants in the study were seldom observed talking about their handicaps or stigma problems in the company of each other. They were preoccupied with these concerns but not drawing on each other for assistance and support.

Dispelling the Conspiracy of Silence

A taboo exists in many settings on openly discussing a person's handicap in his presence. Lorber (1974, p. 120) identifies this as a "conspiracy of silence," which he describes as an unspoken agreement among helping people that the topic of their clients' handicaps is not to be talked about in their presence. It is based on the misguided notion that such discussions serve no useful purpose and may even be harmful, as they may encourage the person to feel more self-conscious and to dwell on a problem that cannot be overcome. Unfortunately, this notion furthers the person's belief that his handicap is so horrible or undesirable that it cannot be mentioned, which only serves to further stigmatize him.

Most people find it difficult to talk about their handicap with others. Obviously, it is not a topic that can be discussed lightly, as it pertains to a sensitive aspect of a

person's identity. In some instances, the study participants appeared startled when they were asked by researchers about their handicaps, and initially some were
reluctant to respond. Nevertheless, they were not so frag-
ile or vulnerable that they suffered from these discussions.
Indeed, they were parties to the conspiracy of silence that
had taught them that these discussions were an inappropriate intrusion into their privacy. Thus clients as well as
staff members may need to examine their resistance to
talking about this topic, particularly in situations when it
can be beneficial to clients.

Promoting Self-Understanding

The topic of a person's handicap is important for him
to explore. It is an important aspect of his identity, which
may impose physical, intellectual, or social barriers to
normal functioning. Mental retardation is not a mono-
lithic condition but a label that comprises numerous physical and mental conditions having over 250 known causes
(President's Committee, 1975). For a person who is labeled mentally retarded to understand his handicap, he
needs to have individualized information about its medical referents, its etiology (if known), the limitations that it
imposes, the extent to which these limitations can be
overcome, and the means of doing this.

The participants generally shared accurate information about their handicaps, but they tended to emphasize
the physical aspects or a specific learning deficiency while
denying a general mental disability. These omissions were
in most cases deliberate because they perceived a greater
degree of stigma to be associated with a general mental
disability. This suggests that another topic to be explored
is the mental retardation label and related issues. The

controversy that surrounds this label was evident in the responses of the participants to the question of whether they perceived themselves as mentally retarded. It is likely that a fairly large percentage of people who are known by this label are privy to the controversies about labels in general and the mental retardation label in particular. Some questions of a general nature that could be explored in peer group discussions include the following:

What do people mean by mental retardation?

Mental retardation is a relative concept. What does that mean?

How does one become labeled mentally retarded?

What's good about being labeled mentally retarded? What's bad about it?

Also, personal questions should be explored:

Am I mentally retarded?

How was this determined?

Who says I am mentally retarded?

Does everyone think so?

How can people tell? How do they show that they know?

Will I always be mentally retarded?

Can I change this?

Understanding one's handicap is a necessary ingredient in understanding one's social circumstances. As stated earlier, two types of problems face the participants, those revolving around their bio-psychological handicap and those having to do with the societal reaction to it. The latter problem area is a critical one. Because people with mental handicaps are encountering stigma promotion in their everyday lives, they need a place to bring these concerns for exploration, examination, and problem solving. Peer group discussion can provide an outlet for expressing pent-up feelings of anguish, fear, frustration, anger, and powerlessness. Help also is needed in understanding particular stigma encounters. Specifically this may include distinguishing stigma problems from handicap-related ones, discerning the origins of problems and the specific motives of the stigma promoters, and analyzing the part played by the client in encouraging or discouraging these encounters.

Managing Stigma

The findings reveal that the participants have developed varying degrees of sophistication in coping with stigma. Some are clever and confident in the way in which they face and manage it while others appear more vulnerable and unprepared.

Four specific response patterns to stigma were presented in Chapter 5. These patterns and others should be viewed as options that can be taken by people with mental handicaps in their attempts to manage stigma. Covering seems to be the most widely used and popular pattern. It has applicability for virtually every person with a mental handicap, and it is noncontroversial. The emphasis in covering is on minimizing the obtrusiveness of a stigmatic attribute. While covering can and should occur in settings where the person's identity is either known or not, there is no pretense of concealing one's identity. Normalization philosophy provides extensive guidance for promoting this option (Wolfensberger, 1972; Flynn and Nitsch, 1980).

Passing, on the other hand, is based on the willful decision to conceal one's stigmatic identity with the intent of gaining acceptance from normals in the settings where one's identity is not known. The issue of pretending to be a person whom one is not is a controversial element of passing that leaves many helping people reluctant to support it, yet it seems that people who pass are most often disavowing the stigma identifiers that are superimposed on them rather than those that are intrinsic to their handicaps. Passing was most frequently evident in the study, for example, as a disavowal of the mental retardation label, affiliations with an institution or community program for the mentally retarded, or associations with a group of people with more stigmatic attributes. When concealment of personal attributes was observed in the study, it seemed to involve insignificant aspects of the participants' functioning. Denial of a learning deficit or physical limitation was not evident in instances in which they could be critical to performance, such as applying for a job.

The moral issue of encouraging a person deliberately to conceal his identity needs closer examination, particularly in terms of the potential negative consequences. Equally important, the part played by the mental retardation system and other systems in creating the need for passing to occur in the first place needs to be examined.

A limiting feature of passing is that it is feasible for

only a relatively small percentage of the people who are labeled mentally retarded. It should be noted that passing as a normal or a less stigmatic person requires both that the person's stigmatic attributes be easily concealable and that he have an aptitude for managing himself in situations where passing occurs.

The pattern of tolerating or encouraging stigmatic circumstances in order to benefit from the secondary gains is another option to be explored in peer group discussions. It is suspected that this pattern is often practiced without conscious intent, and it needs to be examined as a pattern more often having negative consequences for the person's development than positive ones. As was emphasized in Chapter 5, the emergence of the community-based mental retardation system has established numerous service benefits that were previously unavailable, and while many of these services promote the dignity, development, and independence of the client population, some do not. The system sometimes unknowingly perpetuates dependency, stigmatization, and unnecessary segregation while rewarding its recipients with secondary benefits for cooperating. A most challenging task for clients as well as administrators and practitioners involves sifting out the elements of policies, programs, and practices that reward clients for maintaining the status quo when options exist for improving their welfare.

Resisting Stigma

Another option that is available to disabled people is to resist stigma by directly confronting the perpetrator. Most people with mental handicaps may not be immediately equipped for this role and will need assistance in developing the competencies to carry it out. A capacity to communicate anger is a necessary ingredient. In many instances, close associates will have to give the person permission to express his anger in order to overcome many years of social conditioning aimed at restraining it. More specifically, help may be needed in exploring feelings of anger, identifying internal and external barriers to their expression, and learning and rehearsing effective ways of expressing it. Assertiveness training would be a helpful approach in learning effective verbal skills to express anger (Gentile and Jenkins, 1980).

In familiar social settings, resisting stigma may involve confronting the status quo. As the findings of the study indicate, some of the participants wish to break out of traditional client roles that characterize them as passive recipients of service. New roles that involve more responsibility and risk taking are being sought. A few participants, for example, wish to take on a helper role with less experienced peers or to volunteer service to other client populations perceived as being more in need.

A desire to change roles can be manifested in other ways as well. A client in a counseling relationship could want less advice from the counselor and more control over selection of topics and the flow of communication. Clients may wish to assist their affiliate agency in community education drives. Peer counseling, teaching a specific skill to peers, and sharing leadership of rap sessions with a staff member are further examples. In many of these instances, remuneration for the work and role recognition as a staff member or assistant would be appropriate to reinforce the value of the person's contribution.

Becoming an advocate of change is another form of resistance to stigma and possibly the most significant action that can be taken to bring fundamental changes to the lives of people with mental handicaps. Disabled people should be encouraged to become spokespersons for the rights and needs of other disabled people as well as themselves. This advocacy role is particularly important in relation to their client status in the mental retardation system because this system is so central to their lives.

State and regional conferences for disabled people are other important arenas for advocacy. The participants in these conferences are current and previous clients of the mental retardation system, who meet to discuss their common concerns and issue position papers on their rights and needs in such areas as employment, living independently, sexuality and marriage, and problems with stigma. Conferences in several states, including Oregon, Nebraska, Massachusetts, California, and Pennsylvania, illustrate this significant emerging phenomenon (President's Committee, 1979, pp. 53-55). The overriding message emanating from these conferences is that disabled people are experts on their disabilities and must be consulted on important issues that concern them.

In summary, all of the options that can be utilized to manage and overcome stigma should be explored in peer group sessions. These sessions can include presentations of pertinent material by staff facilitators and problem-solving sessions for exploring ways to resolve problems with stigma. Strategies can be shared by more experienced group members, and role play and other simulation exercises can be introduced to rehearse the various ways that a stigma encounter can be handled. Experimentation with these strategies between workshop sessions should also be encouraged, providing material for discussions in succeeding sessions.

An example of a topic for a problem-solving session is how to handle a starer. Beginning with the premise that there is not necessarily one preferred response to a starer, several suggestions could be introduced by the group members. In the study, for example, one participant suggested confronting a starer with the comment, "Take a picture; it lasts longer." Another participant felt that the best way to manage this situation was to ignore the starer so that he "wouldn't get anything out of it." These and other strategies could be discussed, evaluated, and rehearsed to help the group members develop their competencies in handling this type of situation.

LEAVING THE MENTALLY RETARDED WORLD

The option of passing in most or all aspects of life deserves further attention. The metaphor of two separate worlds was developed in Chapter 2 to describe the confined existence of the participants. Their efforts to break out of this confined world are met with resistance both from outside themselves and from within. Special assistance from the mental retardation system to help them disengage from this world is noticeably absent.

Special considerations should be given to the client population that has the potential of leaving the mental retardation system. These clients are likely to be similar to the six participants in the study who are ready to leave it. They may be employed on the outside or preparing for this possibility, living semi-independently or on their own, associating fairly comfortably with people in the outside world, and frequenting restaurants, movie theaters, and cultural events in the community. Their stigma symbols will most likely be minimally noticeable or easily managed and concealed.

Like the six participants, this client population is likely to feel increasing discomfort with their peers who are functioning at a lower level; their wish is to associate primarily with their own kind and normals. Those who work with this client group will need to develop a special sensitivity and acceptance for the growing intolerance that they may have for their lower functioning peers, as it mirrors the intolerance shown by the normal world and may be a crucial ingredient in developing the momentum to leave the system.

Separate programs should be designed for this particular group to help them disengage from the system and more fully utilize services, facilities, and other resources in the community. A team of personnel from the mental retardation system and several generic agencies could coordinate and staff these programs to insure that an effective transition occurs. The benefits of these transitional programs would need to exceed the benefits of the traditional programs that would be left behind.

The group that was codirected by one of the researchers in the study provides an illustration of a transitional program. This group was composed of twelve high functioning clients who agreed to meet to learn ways to become independently involved in community activities. The weekly sessions were used to plan excursions to dinner theaters, sports events, concerts, and other activities. The members decided where they wanted to go, made their own plans and reservations, and chose a companion or two to join them. Subsequent group sessions were used to share and evaluate these experiences and to provide feedback to each other on their achievements. In the meantime, the members were discouraged from utilizing the traditional programs of their agency.

SOME CAUTIONS

Preparing people to understand, manage, and resist the stigma in their lives will not be a simple undertaking.

Resistance will occur in the person, his family, staff, and others. First, the person himself is likely to resist change. His socialization has taught him to function in ways that will thwart efforts aimed at promoting his independence and assertiveness. For example, expressions of anger or criticism directed at staff or parents are a lot to expect. Also, it will not be natural for him to take an active rather than reactive approach to his social interactions and life circumstances. Finally, it will not be easy to give up the advantages of being a client of the system. As a result, progress undoubtedly will be slow and uneven.

Parents and other family members may also be a source of resistance. Even though a mentally handicapped person may not be living with his family, he is likely to have continued contact with them. Parents had the greatest impact on a client's self-perception and attitudes toward stigma when he was a child, and they are likely to have continued influence over him in their current transactions. If parents are overly protective or hesitant to support significant changes in their adult children, they may need help in order for their adult children to assume a favorable attitude toward changing. Parents may need access to professional counseling, a parents' group, or other programs in order to address their hesitancies and resistance.

Opposition may also come from direct service staff members, agency administrators, and others who could be important aides. Staff members in particular may have to do some serious soul searching before they will be able to provide unequivocal support. They should be aware that changes will be expected of them as well as their clients. At times they may be called upon to share their helping roles with particular clients, and their perspectives on what clients are capable of thinking and doing may have to be revamped. Staff support groups and workshops may need to be established to assist staff members in reaching these objectives.

In conclusion, the completion of the study has left the author with new questions to ponder and hopefully these questions will be pondered by the reader as well. Since passing is a feasible option for relatively few people with mental handicaps, what options are left for the others who will never be able to conceal their stigma symbols? Are they destined to remain in a world of restricted associations, settings, and opportunities? Or is it possible to lower the wall that divides them from the normal world? It is the thesis of this text that mentally handicapped people have a central role to play in both lowering and dismantling the wall, that they have options to choose that can reduce stigma, and that non-mentally handicapped people have a significant part to play in helping them.

Goffman (1963, p. 100) suggests that stigmatized people have another option that has not been mentioned: they can voluntarily disclose the stigmatic attributes of their identity to others. This option may be a phase beyond passing in which a person realizes that he respects and accepts himself and feels no further need to conceal his handicap. In this case, for example, a person with a mental handicap would be able to approach a stranger on the street and inform her that he needs her assistance because he is mentally handicapped. A hopeful note to close on is that someday there may be a society in which this option will be a realistic one.

Chapter 7

HOW THE STUDY WAS CARRIED OUT

THIS study was guided by the research of Edgerton and Langness (1978) utilizing the traditional anthropological ethnographic approach. The essence of this method lies in the prolonged and unobtrusive presence of a sensitive and trained observer among the persons being studied. The ethnographic approach is characterized as holistic and naturalistic in that people are studied in their natural context, i.e. where they live. A distinguishing characteristic of this approach is that the field researcher attempts to see the subject's world through the subject's eyes (emic perspective) as well as through his own eyes (etic perspective), i.e. the researcher strives to uncover not only the subject's behavior but also his thoughts, beliefs, emotions, and values, which provide a fuller understanding of the subject. Edgerton and Langness point out that the ethnographic approach more than any other provides a means of reducing reactivity and comprehending the meaning of a phenomenon.

The methodology of this study was also influenced by the work of Glaser and Strauss (1967). These authors, in *The Discovery of Grounded Theory: Strategies for Qualitative Research*, criticize social scientists for placing too much emphasis on verifying theory while losing sight of the equally important function of generating theory. "Grounded theory" is theory that is discovered from collected data. When the procedures of research are aimed at standardization and accuracy of data to test preconceived theoretical molds, the generation of new theories tends to be neglected. This study was guided by what Glaser and Strauss (1967, pp. 101-105) call the "constant comparative method of qualitative analysis," whereby data are routinely analyzed as they are collected, with the analysis bringing modifications and refinements to the hypotheses of the study. The theory generated from the study in this case benefited from the entire data collection process.

Bogdan and Taylor (1975) operationalize the general principles of qualitative research into a specific set of instructions and suggestions for doing such research, particularly participant observation and informal interviewing. Their concepts of participant observation and informal interviewing, while based on sociological research methods, are quite similar to the ethnographic approach of Edgerton and Langness. Their text served as a helpful guide for the research team conducting this study, particularly in response to unexpected methodological questions and problems that arose during the course of the data collection.

OBJECTIVES OF THE STUDY

While the study was designed to explore a range of topics pertaining to the lives of the twenty-seven participants, its primary theme, which cuts across the various aspects of the participants' lives, was the topic of stigma. The primary intent of the study was to discover the forms in which stigma appeared while the participants were at their residences, at work, on the street, and in other settings that they frequented. The design attempted to capture the presence of stigma as it naturally occurred and was talked about by the participants. The study also explored the effect that stigma had on the participants, the ways in which it influenced and shaped their self-images and relationships with others, and their various means of either coping with or resisting this problem. The research questions that the study was designed to answer are presented in Chapter 1.

SAMPLE

During the data collection period, the researchers were in contact with approximately 100 people who were labeled mentally retarded. Thirty-two of them were selected as research subjects, referred to in this text as "research participants" or "participants," and twenty-seven of these thirty-two people remained involved with the study until it was completed. Of the five participants who discontinued, two were consistently unavailable when the researcher was present, one was hospitalized, one chose to withdraw from the study, and one was not able to communicate the type of information that was needed. All of the twenty-seven participants are considered mentally retarded based on available IQ scores. Twenty-two have IQ scores within the mild retardation range and five within the range of moderate retardation. All are of adult age, ranging from twenty-one to forty-two years. None of the participants has ever been married. All of them live in one metropolitan area, four living in the suburbs and twenty-three in the city. Fourteen of them live in group homes for mentally handicapped people, eleven live with their parents or adult siblings, and two live independently.

The sample was selected with consideration given to important demographic characteristics reflected in this metropolitan population, i.e. race, sex, and geographic location. Eighteen of the participants are white, eight are black, and one is foreign-born. The participants are almost evenly divided by sex, with fifteen being male and twelve female. The participants live in all the major sections of this Eastern city except for the central area. Six live in black working-class neighborhoods, eleven live in white working-class neighborhoods, and six live in racially mixed middle-class neighborhoods. Of the four participants living in the suburbs of the city, three live in a white working-class suburb, and one lives in a white affluent suburb.

Consideration in selecting the sample was also given to what seemed to be important variations in the mentally handicapped population relative to mental retardation programming in this metropolitan area. During the time of the study, thirteen of the participants were working in sheltered workshops, twelve held jobs outside the mental retardation system, and two were unemployed. Nine of the participants had been previously institutionalized.

Final considerations in the selection of the sample were the willingness and availability of the participants to become involved in the study and their ability to communicate subjective material as well as factual information. These considerations were primarily exercised during the initial contacts with each participant.

The participants were identified through their affiliation with four mental retardation agencies (referred to as "affiliate agencies"). These four agencies represent a very small portion of the mental retardation system in this metropolitan area. These particular agencies were selected in order to both create a representative sample and include different types of agency auspices in the study. As is indicated in Table II, Agency A is multiservice in nature and Agencies B, C, and D specialize in residential services. Agency A provides an array of services, including leisure activities, counseling, tutoring, residential service, and a small day program. Its clientele totals approximately 160 people. Thirteen participants were selected from this client population, based on representation of the various program units, differing degrees of dependency on the agency, and readiness to participate in the study. The staff of the agency assisted in the selection of these participants. Agencies B, C, and D are group homes, and as Table II indicates, these agencies are located in various types of neighborhoods. The entire client population of all three group homes was asked to participate in the study.

The auspices of all four agencies vary and include a

TABLE II

CHARACTERISTICS OF THE AFFILIATE AGENCIES

Affiliate Agency	Number of Participants	Function of Agency	Type of Neighborhood
A	13	multi-service	commercial area
B	5	group home	racially mixed, middle class, urban
C	3	group home	white, working class, suburban
D	6	group home	black, working class, urban

civic organization, a private profit-making corporation, a parents' organization, and a community mental health and mental retardation center. Another important consideration in the selection of these four agencies was their willingness to permit and facilitate the research work that needed to occur.* All four agencies fully cooperated and often went beyond what was expected to assist the researchers in their work.

RESEARCH INSTRUMENTS

The study, being exploratory in nature, required research instruments that would both organize the data for purposes of analysis and preserve it, as much as possible, in its natural form. A variety of instruments or forms was used to serve these two purposes. During the initial contacts with each participant or group of participants, the recording of the contacts consisted of detailed narratives that reported as accurately as possible what actually happened during the contact. Two forms were utilized, a "Journal of Observations" and a "Journal of Impressions." The first form was used to record what the researchers actually observed, and the second form was used for the researchers' reactions to the contact, e.g. their feelings toward specific people or events, their interpretations of what was observed, any questions to pursue in later contacts, and the effect of the contact on them. The two forms were always used jointly to underscore the impor-

---

*Early in the study, another agency was also approached with regard to its inclusion in the study. It chose to decline because its board of directors felt that the agency did not have clearly defined policy pertaining to approval and monitoring of outside research.

tance of keeping observations and impressions separated.

After an initial period of contact, more focused observations were conducted in order to direct the researchers' attention to stigma-promoting processes. The form titled "Observations of Activities of the Participants" was used during this period. This form included a section for summarizing what happened during the contact, followed by a series of questions to catalog various kinds of stigma-promoting processes.

In addition to the above forms, an "Individual Packet" was kept for each participant. It contained six subsections: "General Background," "Work Experience," "Social Service Utilization," "Formal Educational Background," "Special Collaborators and Other Associations," and "Labeling and Stigma Focus." The forms for each of the subsections served to organize data within these topical areas as the data emerged from observations and conversations. The forms used for each subsection consisted in part of specific questions. These questions, however, were seldom asked verbatim; they were generally intended only to serve as a guide for the kinds of information that were needed. Priority was placed on gathering information with as little solicitation as possible; thus much of the information recorded in these individual packets was either unsolicited or naturally solicited within the context of a conversation or activity.

Another form, titled "Stigma Symbols," was also kept for each participant. The recordings on this form reflected the researchers' perceptions of unusual aspects of the participants' appearance and general behavior.

RESEARCH PROCESS

Methods

Both participant observation and informal interviewing were methods used in this study. The participant observation is most like the "participant-as-observer" type described by Gold (1969). The researchers identified their role and purpose to the participants at the outset, then gradually moved into their activities as participants to the extent that this helped them become inconspicuous and accepted as insiders. They participated in a variety of activities, e.g. eating with the participants, accompanying them to night school and sheltered workshops, joining rap sessions, attending a ball game, walking around town, and joining their dances. In almost all cases the participation was informal in nature and noncontinuous to particular activities beyond one or two contacts. One exception was a formal and continuous participant role for one researcher as the co-leader of a group of clients at affiliate Agency A. This group was established to help its members utilize leisure resources in the outside world independently of the agency. The co-leader role was offered to the researcher and provided him with the opportunity to observe these eleven clients (nine of whom were research participants) as they discussed their experiences in the outside world as well as in the agency. The researcher consciously played a passive role in most of these discussions, with the staff member, the other leader, carrying primary responsibility for choosing topics and leading discussions. Being a co-leader of this group also helped the researcher establish credibility with the agency's clients and provided a context for regular contacts with the participants who were members of this group.

The informal interviews were identified to the participants as "conversations." During these conversations, the researcher guided the participants into talking about the information areas of the study but also encouraged the participants to talk as freely as they wished about whatever they wanted to talk about. Readiness was an important factor in these conversations, as participants were not encouraged to move into sensitive or otherwise difficult topics before they appeared to have reached a satisfactory comfort level with the researchers. The primary realm of interest in these conversations was the participants' subjective state, i.e. the participants' feelings, perceptions, beliefs, and opinions.

Phases

The data collection process was divided into three fairly distinct phases: orientation, focused observation, and informal conversation. The first phase, orientation, comprised the initial two to four contacts with the participants. These contacts usually occurred when the participants were involved in some daily routine activity in which an outsider's presence would not be too intrusive, e.g. a dinner or social event. During this phase, the researchers gave primary attention to a number of issues. Acquainting themselves with the participants and staff was a central task. Rapport needed to be established; thus the researchers attended to what was happening at that particular time and to what people wanted to talk about. A listening ear and sympathetic responses were offered, and general interest was conveyed. Observations during this initial phase focused on such things as the nature of daily routines, rules, norms, attitudes toward outsiders — particularly outside researchers, and the nature of the relationships among participants and staff.

The role of the researchers needed to be defined during this initial phase. In most cases the staff, with prior preparation, introduced the researchers to the participants and explained the purpose of the study. They encouraged the participants to ask questions and emphasized that their participation was voluntary. During these discussions, the researchers shared such things as the kinds of information that they would be seeking; the general intent of the study; the potential personal benefit to the participants, e.g. having the researcher to talk to and accompany them on various outings; the importance of confidentiality; the frequency of visits; and the overall time period of the study. These discussions were usually followed by individual discussions about the study with each participant, in which the participant often initiated conversations with questions such as "How long will you be here?", "When will you come?", "Can you come to my school?","Do I have to talk to you?", and "What do you want to know?"

The second phase, focused observation, was emphasized once the researchers had adequately attended to the issues mentioned in conjunction with the orientation phase. During this phase, the researchers began to vary the times and situations in which they visited in order to observe a sampling of four kinds of activities: staff-participant activities, e.g. meal time; participant-participant activities, e.g. informal conversations in a participant's bedroom; participant-community activities, e.g. shopping; and staff-staff activities, e.g. staff meetings. Specific activities were not observed until the staff members and participants felt comfortable enough to permit or invite the researchers to be present. In time most of the activities of the participants were voluntarily opened to the researchers, but because of time limitations not all activities could be observed. Therefore, priority was placed on those that required considerable interaction on the part of the participants and permitted the researchers to maintain a relatively low profile. This phase lasted about six months with each participant and was the longest phase of the data collection period.

The third and final phase was identified as the informal conversation phase. By this point, the researchers and participants were well acquainted and in many cases had developed close ties with each other. Individual conversations were set up to discuss the information areas that had not yet been fully covered and to give more attention to the area of stigma. The researchers often focused the topics for discussion but encouraged the participants to talk freely and openly. The researchers facilitated conversations with probing questions, and these probes often incorporated previous participant' comments or prior observations that could help focus them on specific areas of interest to the study. This phase consisted of an average of three face-to-face contacts with each participant.

RESEARCH TIME INVOLVED

The study was conducted over a sixteen-month period, involving approximately 400 hours of research time and 172 contacts with participants and staff. The research team consisted of the author and three research assistants. During the first two observational phases, the researchers

were involved in observing eighty-three activities. The
nature of these activities and their frequency are shown in
Table III. In addition to these activities, observations occurred in transport to and from activities, i.e. on the
street, on public transportation, and at gathering places.

TABLE III

NATURE AND FREQUENCY OF ACTIVITIES OBSERVED

Activity	Frequency of Activities Observed
1. Visits to affiliate agencies B, C, and D: e.g., evening meals and post—meal activities	33
2. Group sessions co-led by researcher at Affiliate Agency A	17
3. Supervised activities of affiliate agencies at the agencies and in the community	13
4. Staff and board meetings of affiliate agencies	4
5. Night school	4
6. Sheltered workshops	2
7. Unsupervised community activities, e.g. bowling, shopping	10
TOTAL	83

During the conversation (third) phase, the researchers
were involved in a total of eighty-nine conversations with
individual participants. These conversations lasted ap-

proximately forty-five minutes on the average. They occurred at affiliate agencies, at restaurants, at homes of participants, and on the street. While the average number of conversations per participant was three, the range was from two to nine.

The total number of contacts with the participants by affiliate agency is shown in Table IV. There were considerably more contacts with the participants affiliated with Agency A because of the higher number of participants there.

TABLE IV

NUMBER OF CONTACTS BY AFFILIATE AGENCY

Agency	Research Period	Total Number of Contacts	Number of Participants
A	15 months	82	13
B	8 months	34	5
C	8 months	22	3
D	7 months	34	6

ETHICAL SAFEGUARDS

Several important safeguards were taken to protect the participants and the four affiliate agencies involved in the study. First, the privacy of each participant was respected and protected by insuring that the data would be kept strictly confidential and that discussions about participants would be confined to the research team and research consultants. In the presentation of the findings, caution and care have been taken as well to minimize the possibility that the participants could be identified based on obvious idiosyncrasies in biographical data.

The participants were informed of the general purpose of the study and specific aspects of importance to them, i.e. time involved, methods used, researchers involved, expectations of participants, kinds of information needed, and potential benefits of the study to them and others. After sharing this information with the participants, the researchers asked them whether they wished to participate. They were informed that their decisions would not be binding and that they could voluntarily discontinue participating at any later time. Explicit consent was sought from all of the participants. Information pertaining to the theoretical perspective and research questions of the study was not shared with either the participants or the staff.

Safeguards were also constructed within the researcher-participant relationships. Efforts were consistently made to explicate and clarify what the researcher expected of the participant, what the participant could expect of the researchers, and what was inappropriate to the relationship, e.g. job counseling. Specifically, the researchers informed the participants when they could be available, how they could be reached if the participants wished to contact them, and how they could and could not help the participants with problems. The researchers informed the participants that they would be encouraged to share in decision making about arrangements, e.g. when and where they would meet, what they would do together, what they would discuss, and what ground rules they might need for discussions.

The often delicate issue of ending these relationships was also given special attention. Because the participants and researchers sometimes developed special emotional ties with each other, it was suspected that many of the participants (and the researchers) would experience some emotional loss once the relationships ended. Therefore, from the outset the researchers informed the participants of the time-limited nature of the relationship and near the end of the study prepared them for the eventual ending. In some cases, the participants were encouraged to plan how they wished to spend the time during the final few contacts.

VALIDITY AND RELIABILITY

The design of the study included a number of built-in measures to enhance the validity of the findings. First, seeking data directly from people with mental handicaps precluded any chance of the inaccuracy that often is reflected in data derived from secondhand sources.

Second, because the study was exploratory in nature, the research design promoted a relatively open search for data that could provide understanding about the lives of the participants. In this regard, the seven information areas of the study provided extensive boundaries for data collection.

The design also incorporated measures to minimize the reactive effect created by the researchers' presence. The phasing of the data collection process, beginning with open observation and ending with focused conversation, and the extensive time period that was spent with each participant were intended to create rapport and trust between the researcher and the participant prior to an exploration of the more private realms of the participant's life. As a result, much of the information shared by the participants was in a natural, unsolicited form, and when information needed to be solicited such efforts were usually delayed until the final conversation phase after ample opportunities had been made available for unsolicited comments.

Accurate record keeping was, however, weakened by the efforts to minimize this reactive effect. Only a few of the contacts were tape-recorded because it was not usually feasible to use a tape recorder in the observational situations of the first two phases and by the final phase the introduction of a tape recorder seemed in most cases unnecessarily obtrusive.

Without the aid of a tape recorder, a systematic and disciplined approach to record keeping was paramount. General rules were instituted to promote accurate records. First, brief shorthand notes of a contact were taken immediately following or in some cases during the contact. In the latter case, the researchers usually excused themselves in the middle of a contact and took notes in a private area. Second, a final draft of the record was written within twenty-four hours of the contact to minimize memory loss. Quotation marks were used in records to signify exact recall of a participant's statements, and single quotations were used to signify approximate recall.

The design also incorporated mechanisms to check for reliability. Two researchers conducted the study in three of the affiliate agencies. One researcher was always primary and the other secondary. The secondary researcher was introduced periodically to monitor the accuracy and comprehensiveness of the primary researcher's records by comparison of independently recorded field notes. In those instances in which there was a discrepancy in what the two researchers observed, the discrepancy was discussed to clarify what actually occurred and identify and remove contradictory data. There were only a few instances of contradictory data.

Also, frequent checks were made of the field notes for inconsistencies in the participants' comments and their observed behaviors and for variations in what the participants said at different times while the study was being conducted. Significant inconsistencies were handled in different ways. For inconsistencies in factual information, cross checks were usually made with information available from case records and staff. The most reliable factual source was retained. When inconsistencies appeared in the participants' subjective comments, these inconsistencies were often mentioned during the conversation phase to serve as a probe for fuller understanding of the participants' perceptions, views, and feelings.

While this study cannot be replicated in exact form, the comprehensive and detailed description of the design is intended to create the opportunity for a similar study to be conducted, which in itself can serve as a form of reliability.

ANALYSIS AND PRESENTATION OF FINDINGS

For each of the research questions presented in Chapter 1, a set of instructions and instruments was devised to systematically answer them. Analysis of the data occurred throughout the data collection period, utilizing the constant comparative method of qualitative analysis (Glaser and Strauss, 1967). As categories or themes emerged from the data that suggested similarities in the perceptions and experiences of the participants, more extensive field notes were recorded on these themes so that they could be examined more fully. As more information was gathered about particular themes, particular properties or characteristics of the themes were also identified, as well as variations in characteristics among the participants. These similarities and variations in characteristics were carefully examined as well.

The findings of the study are organized around the themes that emerged from the data analysis process, as each chapter is a presentation of a particular theme. Chapter 2 is an overview of the findings, describing the participants' lives as being confined to a world separated from the normal world. Chapter 3 is organized around the theme of the participants' keen consciousness of their handicaps and the social meanings associated with them. Chapter 4 is a closer examination of the types of stigma promotion in their lives. Chapter 5 describes the various patterns of the participants' responses to stigma promotion.

The findings only describe the twenty-seven people studied. The nature of the research design does not allow for the findings to be generalized to other people with mental or physical disabilities. It is hoped, however, that these findings will provide the readers with new insights and challenges to old mind sets, which in turn will benefit their associations with the disabled people in their lives.

EPILOGUE

Research Participant: *You have to remember that there are all levels, from one to ten. [Level] one has very little wrong.*

REFERENCES

Becker, Howard S.: *Outsiders: Studies in the Sociology of Deviance.* New York, Free Press, 1973.

Begab, Michael J.: Impact of education on social work students' knowledge and attitudes about mental retardation. *American Journal of Mental Deficiency, 74 (6):* 801-808, 1970.

Blatt, Burton: Purgatory. In Kugel, Robert and Wolfensberger, Wolf (Eds.): *Changing Patterns in Residential Services for the Mentally Retarded.* Washington D.C., U.S. Govt Print. Office, 1969.

Bogdan, Robert, and Taylor, Stephen J.: *Introduction to Qualitative Research Methods: A Phenomenological Approach to the Social Sciences.* New York, John Wiley and Sons, 1975.

Braginsky, Dorothea D. and Braginsky, Benjamin M.: *Hansels and Gretels — Studies of Children in Institutions for the Mentally Retarded.* New York, Holt, Rinehart and Winston, 1971.

Bruininks, Robert H., Myers, C. Edward, Sigford, Barbara B., and Lakin, K. Charlie, (Eds.): *Deinstitutionalization and Community Adjustment of Mentally Retarded People.* Monograph No. 4. Washington D.C. American Association on Mental Deficiency, 1981.

Butterfield, Earl: Some basic changes in residential facilities. In Kugel, Robert and Shearer, Ann (Eds.): *Changing Patterns in Residential Services for the Mentally Retarded,* Revised ed. Washington D.C. Govt Print. Office, 1976.

Deutsch, Albert: *The Mentally Ill in America, A History of Their Care and Treatment from Colonial Times.* New York, Columbia University Press, 1967.

Dexter, Lewis A.: *The Tyranny of Schooling: An Inquiry into the Problem of "Stupidity."* New York, Basic Books, 1964.

Dudley, James R.: *Stigma in the Lives of the Mentally Retarded.* Unpublished doctoral dissertation, Bryn Mawr College, 1979.

Edgerton, Robert B.: *Cloak of Competence: Stigma in the Lives of the Mentally Retarded.* Los Angeles, University of California Press, 1967.

Edgerton, Robert B. and Bercovici, Sylvia M.: The cloak of competence: years later. *American Journal of Mental Deficiency, 80 (5):* 485-97, 1976.

Edgerton, Robert B. and Langness, L.L.: Observing mentally retarded persons in community settings: an anthropological perspective. In Sackett, Gene P. (Ed.): *Observing Behavior, Volume I: Theory and Applications in Mental Retardation.* Baltimore, University Park Press, 1978.

Farber, Bernard: *Mental Retardation: Its Social Context and Social Consequences.* Boston, Houghton Mifflin Company, 1968.

Flynn, Robert J. and Nitsch, Kathleen E. (Eds.): *Normalization, Social Integration, and Community Services.* Baltimore, University Park Press, 1980.

Gallup Organization Report for the President's Committee on Mental Retardation: Public attitudes regarding mental retardation. In Nathan, R. (Ed.): *Mental Retardation: Century of Decision.* Washington D.C., U.S. Govt Print. Office, 1976.

Gan, Jennifer, Tymchuk, Alexander J., Nishihara, Aline: Mildly retarded adults: their attitudes toward retardation. *Mental Retardation, 15 (5):* 5-9, 1977

Gentile, Cynthia and Jenkins, Jack O.: Assertive training with mildly mentally retarded persons. *Mental Retardation, 18 (6):* 315-317, 1980.

Glaser, Barney G., and Strauss, Anselm L.: *The Discovery of Grounded Theory: Strategies for Qualitative Research.* Chicago, Aline Publishing Company, 1967.

Goffman, Erving: *Stigma: Notes on The Management of Spoiled Identity.* Englewood Cliffs, N.J., Prentice-Hall, Inc., 1963.

Gold, Raymond L.: Roles in sociological field observations. In McCall, George J. and Simmons, J.L. (Eds.):*Issues in Participant Observation: A Text and Reader.* Reading, Addison-Wesley, 1969.

Gottlieb, Jay: Public, peer, and professional attitudes toward mentally retarded persons. In Begab, Michael J. and Richardson, Stephen A. (Eds.): *The Mentally Retarded and Society: A Social Science Perspective.* Baltimore, University Park Press, 1975.

Henshel, Anne-Marie: *The Forgotten Ones: A Sociological Study of Anglo and Chicano Retardates.* Austin, University of Texas Press, 1972.

Heshusius, Lous: *Meaning in Life as Experienced by Persons Labeled Retarded in a Group Home: A Participant Observation Study.* Springfield, Charles C Thomas, 1981.

Kurtz, Richard A.: *Social Aspects of Mental Retardation.* Lexington, Massachusetts, Lexington Books, 1977.

Lemert, Edwin M.: *Human Deviance, Social Problems, and Social Control,* 2nd ed. Englewood Cliffs, N.J., Prentice-Hall, Inc., 1972.

Lorber, Martin S.: *Consulting the Mentally Retarded: An Approach to the Definition of Mental Retardation by Experts.* Unpublished doctoral dissertation, University of California at Los Angeles, 1974.

Lubin, Robert A. Schwartz, Allen A., Zigman, Warren B., and Janicki, Matthew P.: Community acceptance of residential programs for developmentally disabled persons. *Applied Research in Mental Retardation, 3(2):* 191-200, 1982.

Mercer, Jane: *Labeling the Mentally Retarded: Clinical and Social Perspectives on Mental Retardation.* Berkeley, University of California Press, 1973.

President's Committee on Mental Retardation: *Mental Retardation: The Known and the Unknown*. Washington, D.C., U.S. Govt Print. Office, 1975.

President's Committee on Mental Retardation: *MR78 Mental Retardation: The Leading Edge*. Washington D.C., U.S. Govt Print. Office, 1979.

Richardson, Stephen A.: Reaction to mental subnormality. In Begab, Michael J. and Richardson, Stephen A. (Eds.): *The Mentally Retarded and Society: A Social Science Perspective*. Baltimore, University Park Press, 1975.

Sandahl, Eric: Plastic surgery and a new image for a Down's syndrome child. *ARISE*, December 1978, pp. 5-8.

Wolfensberger, Wolf: *Normalization: The Principles of Normalization in Human Services*. Toronto, National Institute on Mental Retardation, 1972.

Wolfensberger, Wolf: The origin and nature of our institutional models. In Kugel, Robert B. and Shearer, Ann (Eds.): *Changing Patterns in Residential Services for the Mentally Retarded*. Washington D.C., U.S. Govt Print. Office, 1976.

Wolfensberger, Wolf and Glenn, Linda: *PASS 3, A Method for the Quantitative Evaluation of Human Services*, 3rd ed. Toronto, National Institute on Mental Retardation, 1975.